HEALING THE LAND
natural seasons, sacraments and
special services

THE CELTIC PRAYER BOOK

VOLUME THREE

HEALING THE LAND
natural seasons, sacraments and special services

RAY SIMPSON

kevin
mayhew

The Celtic Prayer Book is published in four volumes:

Volume One
Prayer Rhythms: fourfold patterns for each day

Volume Two
Saints of the Isles: a year of feasts

Volume Three
Healing the Land: natural seasons, sacraments and special services

Volume Four
Great Celtic Christians: alternative worship

The hymns in all the volumes will be included in *The Celtic Hymnbook* to be published by Kevin Mayhew Ltd in 2004.

First published in 2004 by

KEVIN MAYHEW LTD
Buxhall, Stowmarket, Suffolk, IP14 3BW
E-mail: info@kevinmayhewltd.com

KINGSGATE PUBLISHING INC
1000 Pannell Street, Suite G, Columbia, MO 65201
E-mail: sales@kingsgatepublishing.com

9 8 7 6 5 4 3 2 1 0

ISBN 184417 109 4
Catalogue No 1500607

Front cover: St Luke and his symbol, from *The Lindisfarne Gospels* by Janet Backhouse. Reproduced by courtesy of the British Library
Cover design by Angela Selfe
Edited by Katherine Laidler
Typesetting by Louise Selfe

Printed and Bound in China

For the Churches and households of Britain,
Ireland and the English-speaking world
from The Community of Aidan and Hilda

Contents

BLESSING THE EARTH

About this book

This is a resource book for new and historic Churches and Christian networks.

Since 11 September 2001 the world has changed and is changing. The Church needs to be responsive as an instrument of a living, loving God.

This book is in the Celtic Christian tradition in the sense that 'the very nature of tradition is that it should constantly change and grow: tradition without renewal quickly becomes obsolescent'.*

With this in mind, the material in this volume is grouped together under these headings:

- Healing a Wounded World
- Sacraments and Significant Life Occasions
- Blessing the Earth
- Prayer Rhythms for the Natural Seasons

---

* Oliver Davies, editor of *Celtic Spirituality* in *The Classics of Western Spirituality* series

HEALING A
WOUNDED WORLD

Introduction

If my people humble themselves . . . I will heal their land.
2 Chronicles 7:14

Healing the land

'Healing the land', to which the Community of Aidan and Hilda calls us, weaves together six strands that have hitherto been kept separate: healing of group memory, conflict resolution, dispelling spirits, hallowing of places, growth in personal wholeness, and healing the earth. Penitent prayer is the common thread.

Healing has to begin with the Church itself

The Church itself needs healing, which must begin in the 'household of God' (1 Peter 4:17). Therefore we encourage churches to make specific acts of healing after careful preparation.

There is the healing of wounded group memory

We are all shaped by group memory and carry it within us. Our group memories may be family, tribal, church, city or national. Memory is a container of emotion, place, meaning, thought patterns, connections. Some group memories may carry such deep wounds that they severely damage the present.

Before meaningful acts of healing can take place, representative people need to engage in a process of discernment that involves 'knowing the story' and sensing the root attitudes requiring healing that the story reveals. This process is sometimes called spiritual mapping.

They then need to make representational confession. As

we pray, we confess as our own the past sins of our group, even if we were not involved at the time the wrongs took place. There needs to be a true sense of repentance and a connecting of the group to sources of healing.

Our models for doing this are Jesus, who took upon himself the sins of every group, and biblical characters such as Nehemiah, Ezra and Daniel, who took upon themselves the sins of their people. See, for example, Ezra 9:6-7 and Daniel 9:4-6.

In recent years people in various countries have been moved to make amends. Japan has apologised for its treatment of other peoples during the Second World War, Australia has held a National Sorry Day for its treatment of its aboriginal population, and British Prime Minister Tony Blair apologised to the Irish for the British Government's failure to tackle the nineteenth-century Irish famine. Pope John Paul II has apologised for the Church's wrong treatment of Jews and women, and Western countries are confessing the sin of the slave trade.

Nations' claims to greatness are related to 'glorious achievements' in the past; claims of revenge are justified by experiences of victimisation long ago. One nation's glorious achievement might be another's victimisation. This has been termed 'selective remembering'. It produces ideologies of denial and suppression. This approach needs one nation to demonise the other in order to legitimise itself. It also creates a fiction (for example, ethnic superiority) which does not fit the reality.

In his Apostolic Letter *Tertio Millennio Adveniente* Pope John Paul II suggested some ways which may help people to live the special grace of a Jubilee Year more fully. The first of these was the *purification of memory*. This calls everyone to make an act of courage and humility in recognising the wrongs done by those who have borne or bear the name of Christian.

The healing process takes into account the victims of each victory as well as the victors. This has been called 'deep remembering'. It leads into reality.

The idea is to identify significant wrong actions in the past that live on in un-whole group reactions, to say sorry and to put right what can be put right, so that we can go into the future freed from dysfunctional group behaviour patterns.

A group of committed people can prepare the way for the healing of a wounded church, locality or nation when its members seek to be free from prejudice, partisanship, blame and paternalism, and are humble and patient enough to learn the story of their locality.

If the members all come from one side of a divide, it is necessary to include some one from the other side, or at least to do as much as possible to build trust with them.

Children can be involved in learning and telling the stories of group memory – both locally and in the wider world – and in preparing and taking part in acts of healing and blessing the land.

There is healing through conflict resolution, forgiveness and deliverance

Centuries-old hostility between groups of different ethnic or cultural backgrounds threaten to tear countries and communities apart. Most conflicts since the Second World War have been of this nature. At a local level this can take the form of gang warfare or mere hostile indifference.

Patrick of Ireland campaigned for slaves and prisoners of

war to be treated well. He fasted against the slave owner who mistreated his slaves. Aidan of Lindisfarne used gifts of money to buy freedom for slaves.

Movements for conflict resolution have grown in recent years. They require participants to learn skills and embrace certain principles. The willingness to listen to the story as perceived by the other side, without judgement or interruption, is one principle. Another is the willingness to share feelings honestly but without blame. Empathy is a third. These principles may be applied to personal, home, church and national life.

Acts of forgiveness can rise up in the night and release a restoring power that corrects the distortion which an act of evil established. A group of Germans who had fought in Hitler's army in Belorussia returned 50 years later to do just this. They built a home for children affected by the Chernobyl nuclear disaster and visited the Chatyn war memorial. One of the group, who had been a prisoner of war, made a deep apology and a Belorussian woman took him into her arms and kissed him. The chain of history was broken.

Michail Fanous and Yehezkel Landau are examples of people who are doing this. They are co-directors of Open House in Ramle, Israel. Here Yehezkel's wife, Dalia, grew up. She was 2 years old in 1948 when her parents, refugees from Bulgaria, were allocated the house which had been deserted by its fleeing Arab inhabitants. When in 1967 she answered a knock at the door, she discovered some of the original Arab owners asking to see round. This moved her so deeply that when her parents died in 1989 and she inherited the house, she contacted the family, the Al-Khayris, and offered it back to them. As they had not been allowed to return and were unable to accept it, they all agreed it would be used both as a kindergarten for the 20 per cent Arab population of the town and as a centre for programmes to reconcile Jews and Palestinians.

Yehezkel, who grew up in the USA, said that he came to Israel 22 years ago because he believed it is God's laboratory on earth, a testing ground to see whether justice and compassion can be the governing principle of a whole society. He says that in a conflict situation it is more courageous to fight for peace than to fight a war. He works for reconciliation between Palestinians and Jews, and also teaches Jewish religion and spirituality in different institutions in Jerusalem. He concluded with the question: 'How can we all take responsibility for the histories which, whether we want to recognise it or not, impact on the Middle East right now?'

Michail Fanous said that his family had lived in Ramle for over 700 years. As part of a minority who have been victims, he said it was easy to hate and to fight. His decision to free himself from the position of victim led him to take first steps of reconciliation with Jews. The Landaus' recognition of his wounds of the past and their invitation to him to be executive director of Open House gave him a practical way of contributing to a new relationship. It also encouraged him as a city councillor in the opposition party to work with a Jewish mayor from the Likud party for the development of their town.

Conflict resolution is needed within as well as between nations. Nicky Campbell asked various Scots on a BBC radio programme, 'Why do the Scots hate the English?' It became clear that past offences still affect the present. The programme stirred to action a young Englishman named Roger Pickering, who had recently married a Scottish woman. On 22 July 1998, the 700th anniversary of the Battle of

Falkirk, he led a group on a reconciliation walk. This battle, made famous by the film *Braveheart*, united the disparate Scottish clans on the basis of fighting the English invader, the tyrannical Edward I. Thus Scottish identity, he believed, was birthed, at least in part, in anti-Englishness. Roger led a group of fasting English people along the route Edward I had taken. Some Scots walked the route their troops had taken. The English made a public apology and they had Holy Communion together. Their desire now is to see English and Scottish people celebrating their differences in mutual friendship.

Children may be invited to think of someone they fear, dislike or feel separated from. They can think of something they can do to show they care about the other person – for example, praying for them, inviting them to a party, sending them a card, or sharing something with them.

Conflict resolution took place among the hostile ethnic tribes in Celtic lands. In his introduction to the Everyman edition of Bede's *Ecclesiastical History*, Vida D. Scudder writes, 'Under the influence of these Irish teachers the spirit of racial bitterness was checked and a new intercourse sprang up between English, Picts, Britons and Irish . . . the peace of Columba, the fellowship of learning and piety, rested on the peoples.'

There can be healing through the discerning and dispersing of spirits

This is an important but controversial subject. Since so many publications address this subject, we limit ourselves to making these few points. St Paul taught that we struggle not only against human foes, but also against 'principalities and powers' in the unseen world (Ephesians 6:12). The Greek word here translated as 'principality' is often interpreted as being a territorial spirit.

Discerning the dominant spirit of a locality can take two forms. First, discerning that cluster of group dynamics that dominate the area. For example, pleasure might be the dominant spirit of certain seaside resorts. Lust or low esteem might be the dominant spirits of a red-light area. Certain places perceive themselves as being on the margins of power, wealth and communications, so they have a spirit of defeatism. This needs to be understood and prayed and loved into transformation. Second, sensing or identifying the character of a 'principality' or territorial spirit that may be cementing or fomenting the negative human mind-set. This needs to be rebuked.

We need to beware of twin dangers:

- Abdicating responsibility for the process of understanding and healing the local community by placing all the responsibility for what is wrong on a territorial spirit.
- Treating too lightly the different planes on which the struggle between good and selfish ways takes place.

Some Christians circle or 'prayer bomb' places and ruling spirits. Others use Holy Communion as a weapon. St Paul teaches that every time a church celebrates Holy Communion they proclaim the Lord's death till he comes again (1 Corinthians 11:26). Some churches believe that they are proclaiming Christ's victorious death to the ruling spirits. Thus, before a service of Holy Communion is held, discernments about the spirits that are hostile or alien to Christ are read out, and these lose their power to bind the area as the Christians partake of the bread and wine.

In the Celtic tradition, seasons of fasting and of prayer and circling of places are a means of cleaning out evil forces. Bede, writing of Farne Island which Cuthbert was to inhabit as a hermit, writes, 'This place was utterly lacking in water, corn and trees; and as it was frequented by evil spirits, it was ill suited for human habitation; but it became in all respects habitable as the man of God wished, since at his coming the evil spirits departed.' They dug through rock and a spring gushed forth. Barley seed was sown long after the time for sowing, yet an abundant crop quickly appeared.

There is healing through the hallowing of places

> Landscape has a secret and silent memory,
> a narrative of presence
> where nothing is ever lost or forgotten.

> *John O'Donohue*

Hallowing places requires awareness of the story and of the spirit of each place. It requires us to walk in the steps of local holy persons, 'who draw to themselves what is earthy'.* It requires us to restore prayer to these places.

The Celtic Christian tradition understands that the divine nature (which is to draw all into co-unity) is perceived in the things God has created (Romans 1:20). God uses natural elements to draw people into harmony with each other and with God.

Each place has its distinctive arrangement of these elements. For example, secluded, fertile valleys draw people because they offer both shelter and life-sustaining water. High places draw people because they offer a vantage point which imparts safety and authority. These physical attributes

---

* Hildegaard of Bingen

have psychic and spiritual dimensions. Thus the ley lines which conduct energies follow the high places.

Such places are holy in the sense that they provide peace, beauty, perspective, or evoke an awareness of the transcendent. There is nothing specifically Christian about these. However, prayers in the Celtic Christian tradition, such as St Patrick's Breastplate, call on the elements to bless and protect human beings, knowing that there is already something holy and powerful present in them.

So when we come to a place of peace, beauty or special memory, we may call on the various physical features in that place to bless the Lord, on the lines of Psalm 148. Each feature of these places may reveal to us something about God's nature.

Certain places are holy because their different parts fit well together to make a whole. Good planning and inspired architecture can provide an urban backdrop as inspiring in its way as a rural landscape. When the different groups, services and institutions in a place relate well together and have a unified focus (that is, they are not a law unto themselves), then there is a measure of 'shalom' in that place.

There are places 'on the edge' such as a rocky peninsular or a poverty stricken slum, which a godly person has made holy in spite of a hostile environment.

The Bible gives many examples of God declaring a place holy because a person has made covenant with God there. After Moses' divine encounter near a burning desert bush God declared this to be holy ground (Exodus 3:5). Sinai, where Moses communed with God, was known as the holy mountain (Exodus 18:5).

The areas around which holy people lived became

hallowed places. Many towns and cities take their name from a Christian who first lived there as a hermit, and drew round them other hermits, or monks, and then families and farmers for whom prayer was work and work was prayer.

The saintly King Oswald and his soldiers knelt in a field where a battle with the tyrant invader was to take place, and planted a cross of wood in its earth. They won the battle, and Oswald named that place Heavenfield. That spot marked a turning point in the destiny of the British Isles. It was the scene of innumerable miracles, and moss scraped from the surface of the cross proved potent to heal disease.

A successor to Oswald asked Cedd, Bishop of the East Saxons, to build a monastery on uninhabited land where the king might come to pray, learn and be buried. Bede records that Cedd chose a site amid steep and rugged hills which seemed better fitted for the haunts of thieves and wild beasts than for humans, so that, as Isaiah says, 'Where once dragons were shall be grass with reeds and rushes' (Isaiah 35:7). Bede explains 'that is, the fruit of good works shall spring up where once beasts dwelt or where men lived after the manner of beasts.'

Cedd was anxious first to cleanse the site from the stain of former crimes by prayer and fasting, before laying the foundations. So he gained the king's permission to spend the whole of Lent there in prayer. This was a custom he had learned from Aidan and the Irish Mission.

There are Jerusalems, Nazareths, Galilees, Bethlehems and so on. Bethlehem is holy because in the simplicity of smelly straw the most holy person was born of a faith-filled mother and saluted by angels. Galilee is holy because its lake and mountains, its spaces and beauty, drew holy people who then drew crowds. Nazareth is an image of a place hidden from public view where spiritual formation is taking place. Jerusalem is meant to be an image of a city where all parts are perfectly joined together in unity (Psalm 122) even though, before and since Christ's presence there, it has become the centre of religious empire builders and a place of strife.

Each place, like each person, has its own God-given charism or potential. The aim of the believer should be to release the place to be its true self, not to copy other places.

In the fourth century Christian Europe came to be dotted with shrines of holy people and martyrs where, people sense, heaven and earth met. The shrines, containing a grave or just a fragment of a saint's bones, were often quite simply called 'the place'.*

Gildas, writing of the Roman Emperor Diocletian's persecution of Christians, observed that 'God lit for us the brilliant lamps of holy martyrs. Their graves and the places where they suffered would now have the greatest effect in instilling the blaze of divine love in the minds of onlookers.'†

Bede records that Germanus, Bishop of Auxerre, took away with him a portion of earth from the place where the martyr Alban's blood had been shed.

Some so-called holy places are really religious places where empire building has a heyday. The holiness and the wholeness which once marked truly hallowed places can be frittered away or overlaid with money, malice or mindless pleasure. The holy places can be destroyed unless the people who live in them get in line with God, as God made clear to the prophet Amos (Amos 7:7-9). In Britain, the

---

* See Peter Brown *The Cult of the Saints* (London, 1981)
† Gildas *The Ruin of Britain* (Phillimore, 1978)

harmony and unity of the old culture were destroyed by the invading Normans, the nation was divided into master and serf, and the land was trodden under. Yet the original hallowing is still buried there, waiting to be rediscovered, and reconnected with the present.

Today people who sense the aura of places are being drawn to sing, play music, prayer-walk or dance in them. Some Christians are called to re-awaken prayer and 'Presence' in ancient holy places.

The mystery of who God is is released into the landscape, which reveals its secrets bit by bit to those who wait, are still, and reflect. To relate in a healing way to the landscape requires reciprocity. The Eskimos, when they kill a seal for their use, pour water back into it. They understand reciprocity.

The value of sacred space is increasingly being recognised. Even if we live in a country without a long Christian history, we can tap into a hallowing process, which is at a different stage in each land.

'New' places can be hallowed. When the astronaut Neil Armstrong reached the moon he placed upon it a celluloid copy of the Genesis account of God creating the world. He was hallowing the moon.

In his poem 'The Hermit', from Part Three of *Station Island,* Seamus Heaney describes a contemplative Christian who cuts himself off from trivial distractions in order that his prayer can revitalise the truth: 'As he prowled the rim of his clearing where the blade of choice had not spared one stump of affection he was like a ploughshare interred to sustain the whole field of force'.

There is the process of personal healing and wholeness

The Service of Healing and Wholeness and its appendix relate to this.

There is healing of the earth

This requires us to relate to the earth as partners, not oppressors; to cherish it, give it rest, respect its nature and its rhythms and to bless it. The Bible depicts the first human as 'Mr Earth' (Adam), a person who looks after and blesses the earth. Human selfishness brought a curse to the earth, and hindered its fruitfulness (Genesis 3). Jesus Christ is named as the 'Second Adam': he comes to redeem the earth and prepare for a new creation (1 Corinthians 15:47-49). This aspect of healing is included in the third section of this book, 'Blessing the Earth'.

Rest is part of the healing of the soil. Most of the farmable earth in the western world is now driven by money. Soil that should have a time for rest, when insects, wild plants and the recuperative powers of nature can have their day, are now poisoned in order to be operative every day and night. Celtic monastic churches kept the Sabbath (Saturday) special as well as Sunday. These were both days for praying, eating and relaxing together. The land and the animals were given a rest, too.

Aelred, in his *Life of Ninian* (chapter 4), reports that, as a result of the local ruler being hard and hostile towards the man who was bringing in God's kingdom, 'the soil seemed rejected and nearest to an accursed thing, since as it drank the rain falling upon it, it produced thorns and thistles instead of wholesome plants'. Contrast Aelred's story in chapter 7 of vegetables sprouting in the monastery grounds, although it was out of season, as a result of the prayer of faith.

Healing through hospitality

In addition to these sin strands in the healing of the land, two further points may be made.

The second section of this volume, 'Sacraments and Significant Life Occasions', may be said to reflect 'healing through hospitality'. This theme pervades the sacraments, household meals and blessings. A strong emphasis on kindness and hospitality pervades the early Christian literature of Celtic lands. Diarmuid O Laoghaire describes an ancient series of Celtic proverbs which begin with the word 'key': 'If the key to justice is distribution, the key to miracles is generosity.' He then cites this poem which is a typical approach to hospitality:

> O King of Stars!
> Whether my house be dark or be bright
> it will not be closed against anybody;
> may Christ not close his house against me.*

There is healing after acts of terror or catastrophe

Secondly, there are prayers following an act of terror and at a public demonstration, with which we end this section. We live in an age when vast devastation can follow a terrorist outrage. This fact could engender despair or hate. It is worth recalling that despite cultural disaster and immense human suffering resulting from plague and Viking invasion, Celtic society and spirituality emerged from the ordeal purified and in some ways stronger. Gathering together for a communal act of prayer cannot remove the loss, but it can provide balm for the wounded spirit.

Conclusion

In 1993 a Harvard Professor, Samuel Huntingdon, wrote an article in *The Foreign Affairs Journal* entitled 'The Clash of

---

* Diarmuid O Laoghaire, SJ, 'Ireland and Her Spirituality', in *Ireland*, ed. Robert McNally, SJ (New York, Fordham University Press, 1965)

Civilisations'. He identified seven civilisations or ideologies that are competing to replace Western capitalism. The aim of Western capitalism is economic growth. This presumes that we are only material beings, and that supplying our material needs will bring happiness. The breakdown in family, and the increase of abortion, pollution, crime and exploitation belie this. The god of Western capitalism is money; its fruit will be division and death.

Islam, which puts God, as interpreted by the Koran, as supreme, and refuses to base its economy on interest and usury, is the chief competitor. It is intent on replacing Western capitalism, which has economically oppressed many Islamic peoples with shocking insensitivity, by holy war if necessary. That is why Iran called the West's front nation, the USA, 'the Great Satan'. This looming clash does not augur well for the healing of civilisations.

The emergence of a global information highway, which respects no national boundaries, makes it impossible for a Western, Islamic or any other nation, to conquer and then barricade itself. The healing of civilisations has to come, not through a territorial conquest, but through communities who live a transforming Way.

This can come about as we learn to weave together these different strands of healing.

> What exactly is healing? It's a mysterious thing, God-given. It goes beyond any mere description of how it happens . . . We are all like islands in an archipelago, all linked below the surface: it seems to me that the immanent God is there, below the surface, the spark in each one of us. I think it's on this level that healing takes place.

> *Susan Howatch*

Healing the Church

The Church exists to be Christ's healing instrument. Yet it consists of humans who have fallen short. Certain actions and periods in the Church's first 2000 years have been a denial of what Christ stands for, and have created negative feelings towards the Church that can only be healed if these are recognised and publicly repented of. Until this healing takes place, the Church is seriously hindered in its ability to heal the world.

The wider Church

Some of the most widespread, corporate sins of the Church have been:

- Mistreatment of Jews
- Mistreatment of women
- Misuse of clerical power
- Buttressing wrong national practices
- Disconnection from the poor
- Disconnection from creation

In England, 'the poor' in some settled populations, both urban and rural, have a grudging attitude towards the Church of England. Folk memory includes clergy who paraded wealth, extracted compulsory tithes, and imprisoned, in their role as Justices of the Peace, hungry rioters or people who worshipped according to their conscience elsewhere than in the parish church.

Following the arrival of the Normans in the eleventh century many churches were male dominated and belittled women and the uneducated.

The local church

Sometimes a church was built in order to glorify the ego of a wealthy landowner or patron, and not in reality to serve God or the people as Christ would serve them.

According to Russ Parker, Director of the Acorn Christian Trust, and a founder member of the Community of Aidan and Hilda, the motivation of the foundation stones of some 1000 Church of England churches is 'You are not wanted'. In folk memory, established Christianity is then perceived as one class enforcing its will on another class. The Church is not felt to be of the people and its dynamic is not felt to be that of love.

Even when some local people no longer remember the historic facts, and when the present congregation is genuinely wanting to serve, the attitudes engendered by the past can be carried on in the group mindset.

During the second millennium, even churches which did not inherit such a folk memory tended to get set and become prisoner to a particular cultural style which outsiders perceived as hostile to them. For example, people from poor housing estates or ethnic minorities can perceive churches to be made up of people from 'the other side'. So churches become part of the problem rather than part of the answer.

At the turn of the millennium Pope John Paul II called on his Church to make penance for its mistreatment of Jews and of women. An act of healing such as the following needs to be carefully prepared.

Preparation

Read Matthew 23:37. What was Jesus' attitude towards his capital city?

Pray for God to give you a similar love for the place you seek to heal.

1. Learn the story of your parish* – the main events that have affected its character and spirit.

2. Learn the story of your congregation.

3. Discern what are the main blocks to the wholeness of the parish.

4. Discern what are the main blocks to the wholeness of the congregation.

5. Hold prayer walks, vigils or meetings at a high place.

6. If reconciliation is required between hostile groups or individuals, seek ways of bringing this about.

7. If representatives of hostile 'sides', or from the past, are ready for this, hold 'a healing the land' service.

8. Form a prayer group which will seek to hallow places, make regular prayer circlings, hold a 'blessing the earth' service, develop celebration of God's presence in the locality.

Where a parish is hardened or fragmented as a result of a mindset formed by events that took place there in the past, those events and that mindset need to be identified and healed.

The Book of Revelation, chapters 1-3, records seven letters which the risen Christ gave to John, one for each of seven churches. He knows them and their locality inside out. A constant refrain of Jesus is 'I know'.

It is best to form a small group of people who want to

---

* 'Parish' can refer to an ecclesiastical unit as in the Church of England, the Roman Catholic Church and the Church of Scotland, or to a civil parish. If the church's natural catchment area is different, this may be taken as the unit.

pray about this, who dig out the facts of the past, and the perceptions of the present.

If heirs to 'the original culprits' still live in or relate to the parish, it is good to talk this through with them, to see if they understand the need for a public act of apology and will be part of it. Bishops, some of whom live in palaces and behave as dignitaries, may also be included in this process.

It is necessary to draw in representatives of the groups who feel disdained by the church.

When the time seems right, carefully plan a public, representative event, which the local population is made fully aware of. Draw up a carefully worded confession of wrongs in the past and an act of heartfelt apology. The reality of this will be communicated if the public sense healing relationships have begun between the representatives of the different groups.

The Jewish act of worship on the Day of Atonement is the culmination of a season of preparation and penitence. Before this begins Jews pray for forgiveness for their own sins, ask forgiveness of any person they have wronged, and, if possible, make restitution. It is good if Christians do the same.

Service for the Healing of the Church

First   Today, listen to what God says: Do not harden your hearts as did your forebears with Moses in the desert, when they refused to trust that God would provide for them. God, who lovingly led them for 40 years, said of them:

Second   They refuse to heed my commands. They are disloyal, and because of this the first generation will never enter the promised land.

First   Today, let us worship before our Maker, who cares for us, whose flock we are.
Echoes verses from Psalm 95

There may be singing

Leader   God's people were called to strive for the ideal of *shalom* – a caring community in harmony with its neighbours, its land and its God. To this God calls us still. Let us pray for our land today as of old they prayed for Jerusalem.

God's Word

Reader   Psalm 122 or 2 Chronicles 7:12-14

There may be a creative activity such as a song, dance, children's display or music

Lament

Leader	Let us say to God:
All	We confess deeds of wrong which cause ills to fester still.
	In sorrow we bring these to you and ask you to forgive.
First	We confess 2000 years of Christian anti-Semitism. Love has not been characteristic of Christianity's attitude towards the Jewish people these last 2000 years.
Second	Jesus said: 'They who take up the sword shall perish by the sword.'
Third	We reflect in silent shame on the Crusades of the Middle Ages when Jews were burned alive in Jerusalem's synagogue by Crusaders singing hymns and brandishing their Crusader crosses in the belief that they were avenging the death of Christ.

Silence

Leader	We also confess with shame:
First	the loss in the Church of integrity, humility and patience,
Second	the crushing of spontaneity,
Third	the caging of the wild Spirit,
Fourth	the breaking off of relationships,
Fifth	the bruising of the crushed reeds,
Sixth	the arrogance of the intellect,
Seventh	the pride of empire-building.
All	Lord, have mercy upon us and forgive us.

Leader   Let us ask God to open our eyes to these wrongs, and to touch our hearts with true sorrow. For this is the path to peace.

All   Give us hearts of sorrow
for all that spoils your land.
Give us hearts of sorrow
for all that spoils your people.
Give us hearts of sorrow
for all that spoils the spirit world.

There may be singing

Leader   If Christianity is to be a force for healing the world in the third millennium, the image of the cross as a sword, by which people of other faiths are forced to convert against their will, must be expunged, and it must become again, as it was at the beginning, an image of unconditional love.

First   From earliest times we have adopted towards the Jews a loveless, arrogant and critical attitude, foreign to the spirit of Jesus. And we have often shown such an attitude to Muslims, to women, and to people of different culture to our own, even to fellow Christians.

Reader   Your life must be controlled by love, as Christ loved us. Since you are God's people, it is not right that immorality or greed should have a place among you. Live like people who belong to the light, for it is the light that brings a rich harvest of every kind of goodness. Try to learn what pleases the Lord. Wives, love your husbands in the way the Church gives itself to Christ. Husbands, love your wives in the way Christ gave his life for the Church. He did this in order to present the Church to himself as a spotless bride, in all its beauty. For we are members of his body.

Verses from Ephesians 5

The discernment group names specific past actions and present mindsets which need to be faced and forgiven. These are confessed in words such as the following:

Leader We confess these deeds of wrong that caused ills that fester still among us.
We confess these wrong group memories and attitudes that still distort and have a hold over us.

Everyone may make a symbolic act of confession such as kneeling before a cross or altar

There may be silent or free confession

Leader Lord, have mercy upon us.

All Christ, have mercy upon us.

Leader May the Christ who was imprisoned and trapped on the tree of life, but who was risen in the morning, forgive us and our forebears their sins, break the power of the past to imprison our present, and set the church free to follow its calling on earth.

All Amen.

There may be singing

Intercession

Reader Make us channels of your peace.
All Where there is hatred let us bring your love.
Where there is injury, pardon.
Where there is darkness, light.
Where is despair, hope.
Where there is doubt, faith.
Where there is sadness, joy.
Where there is death, life.
Grant that we may not so much seek
to be consoled as to console,
to be understood as to understand,
to be loved as to love with all our soul.

Attributed to Francis of Assisi

There may be free or prepared intercessions

Leader May the Christ who walks with the shoes of peace
walk with us on the road.
May the Christ who serves with healing hands
stretch out our hands to serve.
May the Christ who loves with the wounded heart
open our hearts to love.

Service for the Healing
of the Land

For use at any time, especially on 12 July
Suitable for garden and larger gatherings
It may be preceded by folk singing or marching
with bands and banners

Leader   Today let us celebrate our heritage, turn humbly
to our God, seek healing for the land, and reach
out in hope.

All sing   *A well-known hymn or song of thanksgiving*

Leader   God's people were called to strive for the ideal of
shalom – a caring community in harmony with
its neighbours, its land and its God. To this God
calls us still. Let us pray for our land today as of
old they prayed for Jerusalem.

Reader   Psalm 122

There may be a creative activity

Leader   We remember great men and women who have
shaped our land.

*There may be a pause; examples of such people from
different traditions may be read out or displayed*

We remember those who laid down their lives
for another people:
Patrick the Briton who brought Christ to the Irish;
Aidan the Irishman
who brought Christ to the English;

Columba, the Bridge,
who shared faith with all Scots;
Hilda the Saxon
who sent missionaries to other peoples.

Local examples may be given

May we reach out to others in valour and mercy,
weaving a pattern that God will provide.

Fire

A fire may be lit
This may be on a nearby high place to which
people walk or it may be a small barbecue fire

Leader St Patrick lit a fire to celebrate in a new land
the resurrection of Christ.
We light this fire to commemorate landmarks
in our history,
to signify the burning away of all that blots
our landscape,
to be a beacon of hope for the future.

All Holy God, may your purging fire
sweep through our people.
May your blazing fire kindle in us
the flames of love.
May the light of Christ, rising in glory,
banish darkness from our land.

Bread

There may be a picnic, barbecue or simply the following symbolic meal

The leader holds up the loaf, says the following words, and each person eats a piece

Leader   As grain that was scattered upon a thousand hills has become one in this loaf, so may the people of this land become one. God bless us as we eat, and meet and live out the rest of our lives.

Earth

Reader   This paraphrase of the Book of Proverbs, chapter 30, verses 21-23, teaches that certain behaviour creates such dis-ease that the earth itself is affected:

There are four things that the earth itself cannot tolerate: a person who usurps someone in high office, someone who devours what he has not worked for; a person filled with hate who enters a marriage designed for love; employees who have an affair with their employer's spouse.

Representatives of different parts pour earth from containers on to a focal place or into a large bowl

All who wish may place a stone on this mound of earth

Leader   Let us say to God:
All   We confess deeds of wrong which cause ills to fester still.
In sorrow we bring these to you and ask you to forgive.

Acts of apology may be made here

Reader   Lord, for contempt and abuse of others, the
unwanted and the unborn, and for mistreatment
of your creation:

All   Forgive us all.

There may be silence

The cross

*A simple wooden cross which may be made
of sticks or branches is placed in a mound of earth*

Leader   We plant the cross of Christ in this soil which
carries both our pride and our shame.

Reader   May Christ set this land free from the bitterness
of memories, and the power of the past to
control the present.

All   The victory of the cross over neglect and fear.
The victory of the cross over hatred and division.

Reader   Here may healing take place and our wholeness
be restored.

Leader   Lord, bless this earth on which we live
and work and make community.
Take from it the corroding effects
of human betrayal.
Bring from it goodness that will nourish
and renew us all.

All sing   'Christ be beside me' *or another song*

*There may be more singing, a New Testament
reading, a talk or creative activity*

Reader	We thank God for this land.
All	May all that is good flourish in it.
	May all that spoils it diminish.

Reader	We thank God for those who have taught us the Faith.
All	May we hand on a land that reflects more of your kingdom.
	May our seeds of truth and tenderness come to flower.

There may be singing

Healing the Land
Prayers, Actions and Blessings

A candle-lighting at dawn
A candle is lit in a church or other representative place

Reader	Jesus Christ, Light of the World,
	scatter the darkness from this place.
All	You are in this place, Lord.
Reader	Let your healing spring up at dawn.
All	You are in this place, Lord.
Reader	Let your stillness fill this place.
All	You are in this place, Lord.
Reader	Let your peace be here.
All	You are in this place, Lord.
Any	Let your . . . be here.
All	You are in this place, Lord.

The four compass points – a body prayer

Face north. Bend down and touch the earth. Pray for the healing of the past.
Repeat this for each of the compass points.
East: Pray for the present.
South: Pray for the future.
West: Pray for the unifying of past, present and future in Christ.

Bring peace

God said, 'Pray for the peace of the city.'
Psalm 122:6

Leader	Let us speak peace to . . . *(name the place to be healed)*.
Reader	Deep peace we breathe into you.
Second	Deep peace of the warming sun to you.
Third	Deep peace of the pure white moon to you.
Fourth	Deep peace of the shining stars to you.
Fifth	Deep peace of the cleansing winds to you.
Sixth	Deep peace of the quiet earth to you.
Seventh	Deep peace of the knowing stones to you.
Eighth	Deep peace of the forgiving heart to you.
Ninth	Deep peace of the Son of peace to you.
Tenth	Peace, deep peace.

Make a Celtic cross of bricks

The circle in a Celtic cross can represent the area that needs to be healed.

A cross can easily be made of bricks and laid out on any piece of ground, indoors or outdoors.

Collect sixteen builders' bricks. Place six as the main upright section. Use six to make a circle. Place one in the centre of the circle, and one each as an arm above, to the right, and to the left of the circle.

Peace ribbons

Pin white ribbons to each person to represent a hostility that needs to be healed.

Seeds

Plant seeds to represent qualities that need to grow in the locality.

Washing the steps

In Richmond, Virginia, USA, white people went to the Capitol building and washed the steps, emulating Jesus who washed his disciples' feet. They were acting out a parable that they wished to serve the black people who are descendants of slaves.

Stones

Have fairly large stones from different parts of your area. Invite people to hold these in their hand and pray in turn for each area they represent.

Place the stones on a table or on the floor in the middle of the room. Now each takes a new stone which represents something that needs to be let go of. Examples:

- Insults hurled
- Litter dropped
- Cars speeding
- Joyriding
- Brothels
- Vandalism
- Arson
- Dumping rubbish
- Breaking of windows
- Destruction of trees
- Dead people not given Christian burial

Now take white stones. Let these represent a new name, or character that God may want to give in place of the discarded evil.

Storytelling

Tell the story of your wounded locality, but add to it, imagining what happens when Christ makes himself a resident.

Candles

Where there is despair, light a candle of hope, etc.

Healing the Land
Prayer Labyrinths

Labyrinths were a feature of medieval cathedrals, and are making a contemporary comeback.

A 'healing the land' labyrinth can be held in a central, inclusive venue such as a village hall, pub or church.

Use white carpet tape to create a trail with arrows pointing to numbered stopping places where there may be cushions or prayer stools. Dimmed lighting is helpful.

If people with technical expertise are available, labyrinth walkers may be provided with earphones, recorded music and meditation guidelines. Otherwise provide written instructions, based on the following, at each stopping place.

Some stopping places in a 'healing the land' prayer labyrinth

Oneness

A large bowl of sand is placed on a carpet of white paper. Remove your shoes and socks. Place a foot in the sand and leave your footprint on the paper floor. Stand and reflect how every person who has lived in this place has left their print upon it. Now you are making an act of identity with all who have lived here. Reflect how Jesus made a similar act of identity with the flawed human race when he immersed himself in the dirty water of the River Jordan.

Stay as long as it takes for these two acts of identification, yours and Jesus', to sink in.

Stillness

A photo of an ancient local tree, and a log to symbolise a tree, are displayed. Touch the log. Imagine it is a tree that has stood through the centuries.

Be still, with the tree, and imagine what it has witnessed.

Storytelling

This could be a tent. Enter it. Inside key elements in the 'story' of the locality are recorded on CD (use earphones), or are printed out.

Add something to the story from your own knowledge, using felt pens supplied.

Letting go

Next to a container of water is a pile of stones. Take a stone. Think of something that holds the locality back (an attitude or a dynamic). Name it. Let the stone represent this. When you are ready, let the stone drop into the water. From a box on the other side of the water container take a card which reads: 'The stone which blocked Jesus' grave was rolled away. A radiant messenger said, "He is not here. He is alive. Go . . ."'

When you are ready, move on.

Lighting up

An enlarged map of the locality is placed on the floor. A large candle on a stand is alight. Small unlit night lights are placed at its feet, with a few tapers. Survey the map. Think of a place that needs light. Place a night light there and light it. Let it be an image of the light of the risen Christ.

Stay communing with the light of Christ until you are ready to move on.

Ugliness and beauty

Items that symbolise ugliness, blight, or neglect are placed in front of a screen. Projected on to the screen is something beautiful, such as a rose window from a cathedral. Kneel or sit. Beautiful music may be heard if there are headphones.

Meditate on these words: 'I will give beauty in the place of ashes.'

Fragrance

A collection of fragrant oils, pot-pourri or other items is placed on the ground. Choose a fragrance. Enjoy its scent or put oil on your skin.

Visualise spiritual fragrance spreading across the locality and make an act of dedication to God. Depart when you are ready.

Healing the Land
Prayer Walks

Introduction

Prayer walks can take place any time, anywhere. They can range from a few friends who are inspired to do an impromptu prayer walk incognito, to a major occasion that involves the whole Body of Christ in an area, with carefully planned route, music, amplification, etc.

The route may be round the boundary of a parish, village or town. Certain places accrue particular dynamics, through natural force fields, historical association or current use, for good or ill. These make obvious focal points for prayer walks.

The following prayer walk can be adapted to suit local circumstances: Penitence should be made in a place that speaks of dominance. Prayer for cleansing may be said in a place associated with fire, water or cleansing. A high place or building or the town hall may be used to pray for atonement. A place of resource for the neighbourhood such as a park, power station or reservoir may be used to pray for God's refreshing. Prayer for the transforming of sin and suffering may take place at a crematorium, a hospital or at a morally shady area. Praise should flow through them all and perhaps start or end in churches.

Penitence

Scripture meditation: Luke 18:9-14
Confess and repent for the things that have violated or belittled people in the history of the area. You could repeat

the Jesus Prayer (Lord Jesus Christ, have mercy on us sinners) as you walk.

Cleansing

Scripture meditation: Luke 3:16-17

Carry water in a bucket, pray over it, and sprinkle water over significant places with sprigs of rosemary (which signifies remembrance). Or you could take a candle or lantern flame to a significant place and keep vigil, bringing to God things that need to be burned out and purified – wrong attitudes, beliefs, practices. Then go throughout the area praying that the cleansing fire will come to anything you see which is impure.

Atonement

Scripture meditation: Colossians 1:15-22

Walk to a high place or to a seat of conflict with a crucifix or cross. (A crucifix underlines the fact that the Christian God is not, as pagans believe, merely a God of the sky; God has come among us in human flesh.) Meditate on the cross as the place of atonement (at-one-ment) between:

- heaven and earth
- male and female
- a groaning creation and the Creator
- divided families, groups, nations
- the land and the people
- the past and the present

Pray for reconciliation and healing as you walk around the area with the crucifix or cross.

Living water

Scripture meditation: John 4:13-15

Meditate, perhaps in a public garden, on the life-giving waters that come from the heart of God for healing, peace and renewal. Reflect on your baptism. Invite God's Holy Spirit to pour freshly upon you these gifts of healing, peace and renewal. As you wander around the garden, ask the renewing Spirit to bring these gifts to others. Some may wish to take a container of water to bless, and to sprinkle water from this in different streets and places.

The fruits of the Spirit

Scripture meditation: Galatians 5:22-23

Pray that out of the thorny situations that exist the nine fruits of the Spirit may flower. These are love, joy, peace, patience, kindness, goodness, faithfulness, humility and self-control. With groups, each person may take one fruit (perhaps carrying an intercession stick with a colour that represents that fruit), and prayer-walk into the highways and byways of the area.

In churches, chapels and gathering places – praise

Scripture meditation: Isaiah 51:3 ('Put on the garments of praise, O Jerusalem')

Let music and singing, contemplation and praise through creative arts flow in all these places.

A series of 'soaking' prayer walks

In some places a local church may sense that a series of prayer walks around a parish or place is appropriate. The aim is to soak the area in prayer. Each walk has a distinct focus, for example:

- sorrow for past scars
- reconciliation and release
- calling forth potential
- praise
- blessing

From road rage to road prayer

While driving in a queue pray:

Peace to this street, this house . . .

May it be used for good *(for example, for an empty office).*

If passing a road accident pray:

Remedy to the one who caused the accident.

Peace to the victim and support staff.

Old and new high places

The Old Testament refers to pagans who focused their religion on high places.

God-believers recognised that if Good (God) was to replace Bad (jealous, unjust gods) they needed to replace what was unwhole on high places with a true honouring of God and of what God had made.

In our society there are two kinds of high places: man-made edifices and natural vantage points. Christians do well to pray for the healing of the land at both kinds of places. This can be done in an inward but co-ordinated way by individuals who meet beforehand to prepare a common approach. This approach suits buildings such as the London Eye or a tower-top restaurant, where vocal prayer is not appropriate. In a building such as a tower-block of flats, however, it may be possible to pray at the top of the escalator or in a top-floor room.

A natural high place (for example, the Tor at Glastonbury) calls for a prayer gathering with praise music, and proclaiming of Scriptures so long as it does not cause offence to other users. At busy times Christians can meditate quietly, hold up intercession sticks, play suitable solo instruments, or stroll around quietly repeating Scriptures.

New high places can emerge. The Angel of the North is an example of a place at which Christians should pray – it towers over the millions who pass it on the A1 at Gateshead, looks over the industrial north-east of England, and it has a car park.

It is claimed that this is the largest sculpture of an angel in the world, and is seen by more people than any other sculpture. On a plaque at its foot the sculptor, Antony Gormley, states that we need to keep imagining the invisible. He explains that the angel has three functions: to remind us that below this site coal miners worked in the dark for 200 years; to grasp hold of the future; to focus our aspirations and fears. The huge figure's arms are like the mighty wings of an early aeroplane. Christians may see in it a reminder that the early Christians of the British Isles often prayed with their arms stretched out like that, in the shape of the cross of Christ.

Prayers on high places

Leader We have come up to this place to seek a clearer
vision. Here we will envision crops and
communities as they are meant to be.

O God, you are the very centre
from whom all being ripples forth.
Without you the centre does not hold,
things fall apart,
the circle is broken,
the earth ceases to breathe freely,
the water ceases to sing,
the air becomes a menace,
and the beautiful creation becomes cursed.

Here we raise up the Celtic cross –
the circle embracing these violations and the
death they bring,
the halo of Christ's rising from death
that will restore the cycle of life.

In the name of the Christ of the Cross
and the Circle,
we break the power of greed and domination.
We bless what we see, we forgive, we mend.
We call forth life.

A blessing in four directions

Face east From the east – the rising of hope.
Face south From the south – a breeze of the Spirit.
Face west From the west – a waning of war.
Face north From the north – the illumination of destiny.

Hallowing Places

Prayers for any place

Leader   God's blessing upon this place, its men, women
and children.
A blessing on the land which sustains them
and on what is done on the land
which brings wealth.
May no one be in want.

A blessing on its heights,
on its bare places,
on its green places,
on its work places,
on its routes and networks.

May its warming and welcoming sources of
inspiration be as many as the grains of sand on the
seabed, in every nook and cranny of this place.

St Patrick's Blessing on Munster,
a modern adaptation

Leader   You are here, Lord, in this place.
All   May your cross free it.
May your prayers hallow it.
May your peace still it.
May your life renew it.
May your gentleness woo it.

Leader   Let us invite Jesus to make his home in this place.

Leader   Jesus, born in a stable,
All   make here your home.

Leader	Jesus, born of a peasant girl,
All	make here your home.
Leader	Jesus, searched for by wise seekers,
All	make here your home
Leader	Jesus, reared at a carpenter's bench,
All	make here your home.
Leader	Jesus, risen from the wintry ground of death,
All	make here your home.

Blessing a place

Reader	May the sun shine warm upon you,
	the rains fall soft upon your fields.
	May you be held in the hollow of God's hand.

First	The love and affection of heaven be to you,
Second	the love and affection of saints be to you,
Third	the love and affection of the angels be to you,
Fourth	the love and affection of the sun be to you,
Fifth	the love and affection of the moon be to you,
All	each day and each night
	to keep you from fright,
	to protect you from harm,
	to bathe you in balm.

Reader	Psalm 148

First	May the coming of Christ hallow this place.
Second	May the peace of Christ calm this place.
Third	May the cleansing of Christ heal this place.
Fourth	May the power of Christ bring alive this place.
Fifth	May the humility of Christ make gentle this place.
All	May the presence of Christ fill this place.

A meditation

What is the dominant spirit of this place now?

Pause

What most violates its shalom (harmony)?

Pause

What has been hallowed here in the past?

Pause

Where is its sacred/natural/psychic centre?

Read Psalm 79:8-9
Rebuke what violates, bless what hallows

Give us, O Holy Three, your protection,
and in protection, understanding,
and in understanding, the love of all life,
and in the love of all life
to love you and your goodness
in the stream of life in this place.

A prayer on arrival at a pilgrim site

Dear Father God,
I have journeyed to this place and here I pause.
My life so far has brought me here.
My future stretches further than the eye can see.
If, thus far, my journey you have shared,
accompany me now.
Give wisdom, light and always joy,
so that in thought, and gift, and love
my life shall be to fellow travellers
a witness to your Presence in the world.

Ian Fosten

A prayer to say at a sacred site

Thank you
for the life of this place,
made holy by the prayers of the years.
Circle it to keep it holy.
Kindle in the people who live here now
a desire to develop holy lives.

Service of Healing and Wholeness

Introduction

The early Church heeded James' injunction that the sick should ask the elders to pray for them and anoint them with oil (James 5:14). That such a service of healing was carried out among Celtic Christians is suggested by references in the seventh-century *Life of Samson*. Once he found a local chief harassed by a demon. Samson took oil, blessed it and anointed him on the head, face and chest, while many watched. With God's help the sick man was made perfectly whole.

In the Celtic Christian tradition, prayer and practical treatments for bodily, emotional and spiritual ills are seamlessly interwoven.

The girl Brigid fetched some water for her sick attendant and prayed over it before he drank of it and recovered. As an adult, Brigid taught her disciples to make the sign of the cross over eyes that needed healing. For lepers, her community provided barrels of apples; this we would call palliative care.

The *Lives* of early saints such as David of Wales record the improvement of impaired sight after the affected eyes were prayerfully washed or splashed in water.

These *Lives* reveal the sensitivity of those God used in healing. Sometimes this sensitivity was combined with prophetic insight. Cuthbert, for example, discerned that the wife of the law officer Hildmer, who was mentally out of control, would be restored to her right mind as soon as they arrived and placed the reins of their horse into her hands.

Cuthbert himself suffered as a boy from what was probably a sports injury to his knee. A passing horse rider told him how to treat the knee, and, since the treatment worked, the rider was assumed to have been sent by God. It seemed that as a young man Cuthbert, like many of his brothers at Melrose monastery, would die of plague. Yet after an all-night prayer vigil for Cuthbert he shakily rose from his bed and gradually recovered. Thereafter Cuthbert was greatly used in healing ministry, but limped for the rest of his life. He is a sign that the best healers are often wounded healers.

Bede's cautious chronicle *The Ecclesiastical History of the English People* includes a catalogue of healing miracles. Many of these occurred when a sick person touched a material object such as cloth, moss or wood brought to them with prayer from a holy place or person. These are reminiscent of the report in the Acts of the Apostles that people were cured when aprons and handkerchiefs used by the apostle Paul were taken to them (Acts 19:12).

Patience in healing ministry is another quality that the *Lives* reveal. Many a time someone who was thought to have died an untimely death was prayed over and given artificial respiration. Sometimes, as indicated in the *Lives* of Samson and Ninian, this process took hours.

A prayer in the nineteenth-century collection the *Carmina Gadelica* describes Jesus as 'the Healing Man'. All healing, whether medical or spiritual, ultimately flows from God in Christ, who desires our health and requires our co-operation.

> A cause of grief is sin.
> A cause of anguish is death.
> A cause of joy is repentance
> and cleansing in the river of health.
>
> *Carmina Gadelica*

The Service

*A box or board is provided where names of sick people may be
placed beforehand. The service may be preceded by informal
worship, chanting or silent prayer*

Welcome

Leader	Christ is always present when we gather in his name.
	In this service we welcome him as healer.
All	Healing Christ, release among us your power to heal.

The leader explains what will happen in the service

Leader	Christ also walks the world with those who suffer.
All	Healer, we come to you with the wounds of others as well as our own.

There may be singing

God's Word

Reader	Psalm 23, 27, 30, 34, 42, 43, 51, 86, 103 or 121

Leader	To prepare ourselves to receive God's healing, let us forsake those things that hinder it.
	For the ways we have marred your image in us,
All	forgive us.
Leader	For resentment, rush and lack of trust,
All	forgive us.
Leader	Leaving behind our fretful ways,
All	we offer you ourselves in love and faith.

Pause

Leader As Christ removed sleep from the child
who had died,
may he remove from us what impedes our healing.

There may be music

Reader Isaiah 35:3-6; 53:1-5
Mark 1:29-45; 2:1-12; 11:5-13
Acts 3:1-16; 28:7-10
2 Corinthians 3:4-6 or James 5:13-16

Thanksgiving

*There may be a testimony to previous healing,
prophecy or singing*

Intercession

Leader We pray for people unknown to us who are in
broken places of the world.

*There is a pause, or any may mention the names of
broken places*

Leader We pray for these sick or broken people.

*Names, including any which have been placed in
a box or on a board, are read out*

Leader
All Strong God of life,
reach in to their bodies, minds and souls with
your healing love.

There may be singing

The laying on of hands

Those laying on hands stand and a kneeler or chair is placed before them. They join with the Leader in saying:

All　　May the Divine Father make us instruments of healing.
May the Complete Christ take from us all that frustrates healing.
May the Holy Spirit give us the power we need for healing.

Those who wish to receive prayer, or as proxy for someone else, take their place at the chair or queue to await their turn. Everybody else remains where they are in prayer for those being prayed for. Those who lay on hands say words such as the following:

Healers　We lay hands on you in the name of Jesus Christ, the Divine Healer of all, that he may fill you now and bring you to wholeness.

If there is anointing with oil these words may also be said:

I anoint you with oil in the name of the Nurturing God, Father, Saviour and Holy Spirit. As you are outwardly anointed with this holy oil, so may God give you inward anointing of the Holy Spirit to release you from all that binds, to restore you to wholeness, to preserve you in goodness, and to bring you to life everlasting.

There may be brief, silent or spontaneous prayer

Leader   Let us say together:

All   Spirit of the living God, present with us now,
enter your body, mind and spirit,
and heal you of all that harms you.
In Jesus' name. Amen.

*This is repeated until all who request prayer have
been prayed for. There may be a Proclamation*

(When there are more than a few this is
repeated when all have been prayed for)

Leader   Great Spirit, who broods over the world,
restore the garment of our self-respect
and remake us in your beauty. Renew in us

All   the stillness of our being,
the soundness of our bodies,
the secret of our wholeness.

Leader   May we be lit by the glory of God,
filled with the health of God,
always tender and true.

Service of Healing and Wholeness
Appendix

Preparations

Leader	We believe your Son came through death to resurrection for us, yet we find it hard to believe.
All	Lord, forgive and help us to believe.
Leader	We see your Presence sustaining all creation, yet we fear to ask for our own healing.
All	Lord, forgive, heal us and sustain us.
Leader	We pray for the healing of the body.
All	May the strong Lord of life reach into our bodies.

or

All	We confess we have been fearful and anxious for ourselves. We have spoiled relationships with others. Our selfish ways have hindered the world from becoming whole.
Leader	Hear the words of Christ: 'Your sins are forgiven. Come to me . . . for I will give you fullness of life.'

Alternative method of laying on hands

*Those laying on hands go to different places. They
may ask the person coming forward to name any
special need and formulate prayer for this.
When they have finished they may say, 'Go in
peace', and the next person takes their place*

When this prayer ministry has finished, or before if
necessary, quiet worship music is played or sung
and the leader says the final prayer

For those who desire healing
of a lack of self-worth

Leader   We pray for healing of distorted self-image.
All   We grieve that we hurt others and have been
     hurt ourselves, that we hide our wounds
     and are afraid of being vulnerable.
     Help us to come to you as we are,
     and to receive all that you wish to give us.

Healers   Always a mind has desired you,
     an eye has seen you,
     a mouth has named you,
     a heart has desired you.

All   We receive the power of the Creator of life,
     we receive the power of the Christ of love,
     we receive the help of the Holy Spirit,
     who together bring us to wholeness.

For those who desire healing
of drivenness

All   We are sorry, O Lord, for
     dis-ease in our eyes – we have been driven
     in our looking;
     dis-ease in our ears – we have been driven
     in our listening;
     dis-ease in our tongues – we have been driven
     in our speaking;

dis-ease in our heart – we have been driven
in our loving,

Leader   'Be still and know that I am God . . .
I am the Lord who heals you . . .'

For those who wish to forgive
another person

Leader   Imagine the person who needs your forgiveness
standing in front of you. Jesus is standing behind
them with his arms round their shoulders.
Clearly, Jesus loves this person you resent and
is asking you to forgive them. In this moment
of silence you may wish to tell them how much
they have hurt you, knowing you can do so
in complete confidence.

Short silence

Forgivers In the name of our Lord Jesus Christ,
I forgive you from my heart
for the hurt you have caused me.
I release you and call down the peace
and blessing of God upon you;
and I thank God that you are forgiven.

Covenant Service

This weaves together Celtic elements with the Methodist covenant service established by John Wesley.

It links the covenants God made with the earth through Noah, with a nation through Moses, and with all people through Abraham and Christ.

It may be used at the beginning of an educational, church or national year.

There may be singing

Leader Today we renew our covenant with God,
as our forebears in faith have done
through the generations.

Leader The beauty of the rainbow
in the arching sky;
All beautiful too visiting the ones we love.
Leader The beauty of fish
in the shimmering water;
All beautiful too covenant with the Creator.
Leader The beauty of the word
with which the Trinity speaks;
All beautiful too doing penance for sin.
Leader But the loveliest of all is covenant with God
on the Day of Judgement.
All Amen.

Echoes The Loves of Taliesin

God's Word

Reader	Psalms 66 or 90
Leader	We bless you for your covenant with Noah.
All	Renew our relationship with the earth, and all that live by it.
Leader	We bless you for your covenant with Moses.
All	Renew our relationship with the human community.
Leader	We bless you for your covenant with David.
All	Renew our relationship with the royal priesthood of the Church.
Leader	We bless you for your covenant with Jesus.
All	Renew our relationship with the Defenceless Love who draws the whole created world to himself.

The story of Noah may be told (Genesis 6-9)
or the following may be read:

Reader	Jeremiah 31:31-34
Leader	We adore you, gracious Father, that you have revealed your glory in the incarnation of your Son.
All	Blest be God for ever.
Leader	We adore you, gracious Jesus, for being our pattern of goodness whose light shines across the world.
All	Blest be God for ever.
Leader	We adore you, Holy Spirit, that you transform everyday things until they reflect the glory of God.
All	Blest be God for ever.

There may be singing

Reader	Hebrews 12:18-29 or John 13:33-35

Confession of sin

Leader   God our Creator, you called the human race
to tend and bless your creation:
we confess with shame that we have neglected
and misused it for our selfish ends.

All   Have mercy on us, and forgive.

Leader   God our Teacher, you revealed your laws that alone
enable us to live in well-being and mutual respect:
we confess that we have fallen prey to prejudice,
greed and dishonest ways.

All   Have mercy on us, and forgive.

Leader   God our Saviour, you have shown us
the true way of life in your loved Son:
we confess with shame that we are slow to learn
of him, fail to heed him, and are reluctant
to follow his way of the Cross.

Leader   God our Lover, we confess that our worship is
threadbare; we neglect the means of your
blessing; we evade our responsibilities in the
Body of Christ; we are imperfect stewards of
your gifts and imperfect witnesses to Christ.

All   Have mercy on us, and forgive us.

Leader   Let each of us in silence make our own
confession to God.

Silence

All   Have mercy on me, O God. In your unfailing
love cancel my offences, and wash me completely
from my sin. Create in me a clean heart.

A minister declares Christ's forgiveness of sins

The covenant

All stand

Leader Let us place ourselves under Christ.
This means that we are happy for him to give us
our place and work,
and that he himself is our reward.
Christ has many tasks to be done;
some are easy,
others are difficult;
some bring honour,
others bring reproach.
In some we may please Christ and please ourselves,
in others we cannot please Christ
except by denying ourselves.
Yet the power to do all these things
is given us by Christ who gives us strength.
Therefore let us give ourselves afresh to him,
trusting in his promises and relying on his help.

All Lord, with joy we pledge our love of you.
We are no longer our own, but yours.
Put us to what you will,
place us with whom you will;
let us be put to work for you or put aside for you;
let us be full, let us be empty;
let us have all things, let us have nothing.
We freely and with all our heart
give you all things for you to use.
May we walk through this year in unity
with you and our fellow Christians,

feeding upon your Word,
honouring all people,
cherishing your creation,
serving our neighbour,
responsive to the leading of your Spirit.

*There may be teaching, creative activity, sharing,
eating or singing*

Intercession

Reader   In the steep common path of our calling,
whether it be easy or uneasy to our flesh,
whether it be bright or dark for us to follow,
may your own perfect guidance be given us.
Be a shield to us from the ploys of the deceiver,
and in each hidden thought
our minds start to weave
be our director and our canvas.

Carmina Gadelica

There may be prepared or free prayer and singing

Leader   May we be bold in the love of God,
strong in the peace of God,
rich in the mercy of God.

Brian Frost

Creative activity

*Each person may bring a Bible and lay it on an
altar or table. They place their hand upon it as
they say their solemn words of covenant.*

Transfiguration
Candle-lighting

The following candle-lighting and pattern of worship may be used at any time, and especially on the Feast of the Transfiguration, 6 August. That is also the date the first atomic bomb was dropped on Hiroshima in 1945. So we not only recall the transfiguration of Christ before his death but also pray for the transfiguration of the scarred creation.

For use in a household or before the Pattern of Worship that follows

A candle is lit

Leader Jesus Christ is the Light of the World,
shining here among us.

Leader When Peter and his two friends
were on a mountain with Jesus
they awoke from a sleep
to see Christ transfigured by light.

All Awaken us to your glory.

First Restore our seeing.
All Awaken us to your glory.

Second Steer us towards our destiny.
All Awaken us to your glory.

First Cure our deafness.
All Awaken us to your glory.

Second Stir us to adventure.
All Awaken us to your glory.

Leader Since we have this cloud of witnesses, including Moses and Elijah who were manifested on the mountain with Jesus, let us rid ourselves of everything that gets in the way, and of the sin which clings to us so tightly, and let us run with determination the race that lies before us. Let us keep our eyes on Jesus, on whom our faith depends from beginning to end.

Adapted from Hebrews 12:1-2

There may be singing

Lament

First Christ and his garments were transfigured on a mountain to strengthen him before he went to his torture and death at Golgotha.

Second The atomic bomb dropped on Hiroshima, and a second on Nagasaki, killed and radiated Christians, as well as many others, who were like lambs brought to the slaughter.

All Jesus, Lamb of God, have mercy on us.

First Suppose the material order is the body of the Divine Christ. We took his body and we enacted a Cosmic Golgotha. We took the key to love and used it to unlock hell.

*There may be music of lament
while the following is said and enacted:*

Second We grieve for the destruction wrought on this world, for the tearing of limbs and of land.

We bleed for the smashing of homes and of
hearts, the scorching of earth and of hope.

All   Lord, heal our world, forgive our madness,
have mercy on your blinded children.

*A globe may be placed in the centre and
designated persons encircle it, placing their
hands on or around it in prayer.
When the music ends, they return to their places*

Intercession

First   When we face devastation and suffering
make us aware, all merciful God,
of the eye that beholds us,
the hand that holds us,
the heart that loves us,
the Presence that enfolds us.

Second   When the earth is scorched
and all creation groans,
make us aware, all merciful God,
that you can transfigure its very atoms
and elements.

Leader   We pray for groaning parts of your creation:

Examples may be given

Leader   Transfigure this earth:
may people and animals be friends on it;
may the scarred places be healed on it;
may our bodies be resurrected on it.

There may be teaching, creative activity and singing

Morning Prayer for Transfiguration

Leader   Mighty king, you summon the dawn.
All   In your light shall we see light.
Leader   On a mountain you revealed your glory
              and filled the disciples with awe.
All   In awe we come to you.

There may be singing

Reader   Psalm 8

*A candle or incense may be lit or there may be
more singing*

God's Word

Reader   *2 Chronicles 5:11-14*
              The Levites stood near the east side of the temple
              altar with cymbals and harps, and with them were
              a hundred-and-twenty priests playing trumpets.
              The singers were accompanied in perfect harmony
              by trumpets, cymbals, and other instruments, as
              they praised Yahweh singing: 'We praise you
              Yahweh, because you are good, and your love is
              eternal.' As the priests were leaving the temple it
              was suddenly filled with a cloud shining with the
              dazzling light of the Divine Presence, and they
              could not continue the service of worship.

              *There may be a pause, music, or group dance
              that celebrates the use of the body to glorify God*

Leader	Almighty God, Creator, greyness has enveloped our world.
All	As we lift our hearts to you may your glory make all things clear.
Leader	Almighty God, Creator, you seem absent from your world.
All	Sun of suns, in everything we touch and everyone we meet, light up for us your presence.
Leader	Almighty God, Creator, awaken to us your presence in cloud and grey and storm,
All	till our trivial tasks become sacraments in the temple of your love.
Reader	Luke 9:28-36

Intercession

Leader	Your kingdom come on earth, as it is in heaven.
All	Transfigure this earth.
Females	May flowers bloom on it.
All	Transfigure this earth.
Males	May peace reign on it.
All	Transfigure this earth.
Females	May people and creatures be friends on it.
All	Transfigure this earth.
Males	May our bodies be changed into bodies of resurrection.
All	Transfigure this earth.

There may be singing, teaching or creative activity

Leader	Jesus, you took your friends to be alongside you.
All	May we stay close to you today.

There may be silent or spoken adoration

Leader   Father, you transfigured your Son
to strengthen him for his coming trial.

All   Strengthen us in our trials.

A pause to recall any trials we may face

Leader   Spirit, your glory encompassed them
on the mountain.

All   Encompass us with your glory.

*There may be singing and any of the following
prayers may be used*

Leader   Saviour, you led the disciples down to serve
a suffering world.

All   Have mercy on the suffering world today.

*There may be a pause or any one may name
examples of suffering in the world*

First   We pray that into blighted places
you will bring communities of light . . .

Second   We pray that into unvisited places
you will bring sanctuaries of prayer . . .

Third   We pray that unto disheartened believers
you will reveal the Resurrection . . .

Fourth   We pray that those who have been disfigured
by atomic blast will be transfigured . . .

Fifth   We pray for the redemption
of the whole creation and for an end to the
needless suffering of animals . . .

Leader   Make me aware, Lord,
of the eye that beholds me,
the hand that holds me,
the heart that loves me,
the Presence that enfolds me.

All   May the face of the Father of glory,
the face of the Sun of suns,
the face of the radiant Spirit,
pour light upon us throughout this day.

Midday Prayer for Transfiguration

Leader   Glory to God above,
glory to Christ beside,
glory to the Spirit within.
Lord come and put a glory in my work today.
Come and put a shine on the noontime fray.
May the Glory come now from the heavens high,
the Glory come to me; the Glory come nigh.

Reader   Jesus took Peter, James, and John, the brother
of James, to a high mountain where they were
alone; and in their presence he was transfigured.

There may be singing or the lighting of a candle

Leader   Jesus, transfigured on a mountain,
you took your friends down to the valley
of everyday life.

All   Be with us in the midst of this day.

Leader   Jesus, in the midst of the day
you were stretched out on the Tree of Death;
the elements erupted and the earth was
transfigured.

All   Transfigure us in the midst of the day.

There may be silence or free prayer

Reader   There are varieties of work, but the same Spirit
gives work for everyone to do. Each person is
given a gifting of God's Spirit to use for the
common good.   *1 Corinthians 12:4, 5*

Leader	Your glory be seen in work that is done from the heart.
All	Your glory be seen in work that meets true needs.
Leader	Your glory be seen in communication that ennobles the spirit.
All	Your glory be seen in beauty of form and friendship.

*There may be a pause before and between
the following sentences*

Reader	Your glory be seen in the stature of waiting . . . Your glory be seen in the grace of unknowing . . . Your glory be seen in the dignity of humbling.
All	We reflect like mirrors the glory of the Lord. The Lord, who is the Spirit, transforms us in ever-increasing glory into God's image.

2 Corinthians 3:18

Leader	The glory of God in my working.
All	The glory of God in my thinking.
Leader	The glory of God in my speaking.
All	The glory of God in my eating.
Leader	The glory of God in my hearing.
All	The glory of God in my meeting.

There may be singing, sharing or silence

Leader	Glorious Three, shine upon our tired and drooping hearts. Complete the work to which you have called us. Pour lovingly and generously upon us hour by hour.

Evening Prayer for Transfiguration

Leader You led your people to a place
of shining brightness;
may the light of your Presence shine on us.

All Lord of glory, it is good that we are here.

There may be singing

God's Word

Reader Psalm 56

All Response after verse 4, 7, 11 and 13:
I walk in the presence of God,
in the light that shines on the living.

Leader You revealed your glory in the face of Christ,
you confirmed your disciples in their faith, you
gave a foretaste of the victory of your kingdom.

All Your kingdom come on earth, as in heaven,
for the kingdom, the power and the glory
are yours, now and for ever. Amen.

Reader Exodus 34:29-35

All Eternal Light, shine into our hearts.
Eternal Goodness, deliver us from evil.
Eternal Wisdom, scatter the darkness
of our ignorance,
help us ever to seek your face.
Until you bring us into your holy Presence.

Alcuin

Reader 2 Peter 1:10-19

Lament

Leader Truth and holiness shine through your saints.
All Forgive us for the parts of our lives
that are false or frozen.
Leader The Saviour and the saints are radiant and
fruitful.
All Take from us all that clouds the soul.
Leader Jesus, to your dispirited disciples
you revealed the Resurrection.
All Arm us with the joy of victory.

There may be silence, singing or sharing

Intercession

Leader You are here, Lord, in this place.
All Transfigure and heal us.
Leader We set our faces steadfastly
towards your purpose for us.
All Transfigure and heal us.
Leader We include in our prayer the sick and suffering
whom we shall meet.
All Transfigure and heal us.
Leader We remember that on this day
the atomic bomb was dropped on Hiroshima;
we stand with those who died and those who
are still in pain.
All Transfigure and heal us.

Leader   We remember Moses and Elijah,
              witnesses of life triumphant over death
              and we think of all the faithful departed.

All   Transfigure and heal us.

There may be silence or free prayer

Leader   Reveal your Presence, enchant our hearts,
              and shine on our acquaintances.

All   May the Lord bless us and keep us,
              may Christ smile upon us and change us,
              may he unveil his face and keep us in peace.

Night Prayer for Transfiguration

Leader   We come into
the presence of the Creator who made us,
the Son who transforms us,
the Spirit who renews us.

Reader   Psalm 8 or another Psalm may be read.

A candle may be lit. There may be singing or music

Reader   Jesus took Peter, James and John
up a mountain to pray. As he was praying
he was transfigured before them; his face
shone like the sun, and his clothes
became sparkling white.

From Luke 9 and Matthew 17

Leader   You are our Saviour and Lord,
All   in our darkness be our Light.
Leader   May the things that cloud our vision flee:
All   envy, unbelief and strife.

Leader   It was on the day of the Transfiguration
that the first atomic bomb was dropped
on Hiroshima, so enacting a Cosmic Golgotha;
therefore let us pray to the transfiguring God
whose Christ is the first fruit of a new creation.

Leader   We bring to you creation in its pain,
All   transfigure creation in its pain.
Leader   We bring to you the creatures and the soil,
All   transfigure the creatures and the soil.

Leader We bring to you our tiredness and our toil,
All transfigure our tiredness and our toil.

Leader This night we pray
for the disfigured on earth, the sick,
the dying and victims of nuclear explosion

There may be silent or free prayer

Leader This night we also pray for our dear ones;
let us name them aloud or in silence . . .

Any *(Dear ones may be named)*

Leader As the sun sets on this your world,
All bathe us in your glory
and bring us to the gates of heaven.

Leader I lie down this night
with the King of Life,
with the Christ of transfiguration,
with the Holy Spirit –
and with the angels
from the crown of my head
to the soles of my feet;
All from the crown of my head
to the soles of my feet.

There may be singing

Leader May the eternal Glory shine upon us,
may the Son of Mary stay beside us,
may the peace-giving Spirit dwell within us,
All may the radiant Three light up our night.

Creative activities

- Burn incense to represent the cloud that covered Christ on the mountain.
- Put on white garments.
- Display pictures or icons of Moses and Elijah and Christ.

Sanctity of Life

This may be used at any time, and especially on 28 December, traditionally known as Holy Innocents' Day, which commemorates the day King Herod ordered every male infant in the locality of Jesus' birth to be killed.

Leader   The Word of God has been born as a human being, full of grace and truth.
In him is life, and the life is the light of all people.
The light still shines in the darkness.

One candle or the five candles of the Advent-Christmas wreath are lit

Leader   Jesus Christ is the Light of the World:
All   a light that no darkness can quench.

There may be singing

Leader   Today we recall how the tyrant King Herod, hearing of Jesus' birth in Bethlehem, ordered all the infant boys there to be killed; we trace the victory of the Light of the World over the powers of darkness, and we pray for the sanctity of life to be protected in our time.

Lament

Leader   Jeremiah, who lived centuries before Christ, prophesies about some descendants of Rachel, who was buried at Bethlehem, near Ramah:
'The voice of bitter lament is heard in Ramah.

Rachel is weeping for her children, because they are no more.'

Jeremiah 31:15

Reader We too weep, for the unborn and newly born whose lives have been cut short, and for the mutilation and death of innocent millions through neglect and war.

Reader Lord, for contempt and abuse of others, for failure to protect the lives of the unwanted and the unborn, and for mistreatment of your creation:

All forgive us all.

Reader Lord, we thank you for the example of Mary who bore your Son in her womb and suffered persecution of her newborn child. Inspire parents, health workers and us all to provide genuine love to every infant, whatever the conditions they are born into.

God's Word

Reader Matthew 2:13-21

*There may be teaching, sharing, and singing
The words below may be read:*

Reader You're special.
In all the world there is nobody, nobody like you.
Since the beginning of time there has never been another person like you.
Nobody has your smile, your eyes, your hands, your hair.

Nobody owns your handwriting, your voice.
You're special.
Nobody can paint your brush strokes.

Nobody has your taste for food or music,
or dance or art.
Nobody in the universe sees things as you do.
In all time there has never been anyone
who laughs in exactly your way,
and what makes you laugh or cry or think
may have a totally different response in another.
So – you're special.
You are different from any other person
who has ever lived in the history of the universe.
You are the only one in the whole creation
who has your particular set of abilities.
There is always someone who is better
at one thing or another.
Every person is your superior in at least one way.
Nobody in the universe can reach the quality
of the combination of your talents, your feelings.
Like a roomful of musical instruments
some might excel in one way or another,
but nobody can match the symphonic sound
when all are played together. Your symphony.
Through all eternity no one will ever walk, talk,
think or do exactly like you. You're special . . .
God made you for a special purpose.
He has a job for you to do that nobody else
can do as well as you can.
Out of the billions of applicants
only one is qualified.

Only one has the unique and right combination
of what it takes, and that one is you.
You're special.   *Anon*

*Alternate verses of the following Psalm may be read
by a male and a female, and there may be singing*

Reader   Psalm 8

Intercession

*Prayers for specific needs may be prepared by a
reader or groups to follow each intercession below,
or these may be followed by free prayer*

Leader   High King of the universe,
by choosing to be born as a child
you teach us to reverence every human life.
May we never despise, degrade or destroy it.
Rather, help us sustain and preserve it.

Reader   We pray that every person may be cherished
from conception to the grave . . .
We pray for unborn children, for their mothers
and all who have care of them . . .
We pray for those with physical handicaps to be
encouraged to transcend them . . .
We pray for those who make laws, educate
and provide health care,
that they may cherish every human life . . .

There may be silence, music, sharing or singing

Leader   God bless the earth beneath us,
each life that is around us,
your image deep within us.

Commonwealth Observance

*Suitable for use on Commonwealth Day,
the second Monday in March, or at any time*

The Commonwealth is a unique global family of 54 member countries. From a club of former colonies of one of the Celtic nations (Britain), it has grown into a modern international association. Committed to racial equality and national sovereignty, the Commonwealth became a natural association of choice for many new nations emerging out of decolonisation in the 1950s and 1960s.

With English as a common working language and similar systems of law, public administration and education, today it helps to advance democracy, human rights, and sustainable economic and social development.

From Africa to Asia, from the Pacific to the Caribbean, from Europe to North America, the 1.7 billion people of the Commonwealth make up a quarter of the world's population. Over half of the Commonwealth's peoples are aged 25 or under. The Commonwealth is served by a Secretariat. For historical reasons it retains as its head the non-political British sovereign as a symbol of continuity and unity in diversity.

Introduction

Leader   Light of the World, whose rays have lit up every land, we celebrate the good things of our past, and our commonwealth of human fellowship.

There may be singing

Leader   Let us give thanks for blessings we have enjoyed.

Representatives of each country may give thanks,
verbally or visually, for a blessing given to their land

At the close, a long note of a horn or similar
instrument may be played

Lament

Reader   Who shall pass into the holy presence of God?
Those who have clean hands and pure hearts.

Psalm 24:3-4

Reader   Let us acknowledge that not one of our
countries is without imperfections; we have all
fallen short of the ideals we proclaim.
All   Lord, have mercy upon us.

Reader   Let us recall the things that stain our memories;
the complaining and grasping spirit, the me-first
attitude, the unfair practices, the hostility
towards others, the contempt for divine laws
and humane values.

There may be silence or representatives may give
examples from their own countries

Reader   For these and all our sins, forgive us, merciful God.
All   Amen.

God's Word

Either

First Listen to these words the Compassionate,
the Merciful, the Almighty God has given to all
people: Love the Lord your God with all your
heart, with all your soul, with all your mind
and with all your strength . . . Honour your
father and mother. Do not commit murder.
Do not take another's spouse. Do not steal.
Do not be a false witness. Do not covet.
Love your neighbour as yourself.

Echoes the Torah

Second We have divided you into nations and tribes that
you may get to know one another. The noblest
of you in the sight of the All-wise and All-
knowing is the one who reverences him most.

Koran 49

Third Respect all people.

Jesus

Fourth Do not allow hatred to turn you away
from justice.   *Koran 5*

Fifth Forgive those who persecute you.

Jesus

Sixth In the Torah we decreed a life for a life. But if
a person out of love holds back from retaliation,
this forbearance will make up for their other sins.

Koran 5

Seventh   From the unreal lead us to the Real.
From darkness lead us to light.
From death lead us to immortality.

Hindu

or

Reader   1 Kings 8:54-end

Silence or singing

Leader   Lord God almighty, King of the nations,
All   how right and true are your deeds.
Who will refuse to declare your greatness?
You alone are holy.
All the nations will come and worship you
because your just actions are seen by all.

Revelation 15:3-4

Reader   Matthew 22:15-22

*There may be talks, creative activities, presentations
and singing*

The Celtic Commonwealth Cross

*A large Celtic Cross is carried in to the accompaniment of music.
Representatives of Commonwealth countries form a circle,
standing or dancing with arms reaching out. Other representatives kneel to form the shape of a cross inside the circle. The
music stops and the representatives say the following prayer:*

Circle us, O God.
Keep good within, keep harm without.
Circle us, O God.

Keep generosity within, keep greed without.
Circle us, O God.
Keep love within, keep hate without.
Four more representatives run in. One of them asks:

Representative

Haven't you all forgotten something?
The people who lived and struggled before us
and who gave their lives are also part of the
Commonwealth circle.

*Each of the four representatives
joins the four Cross lines so that each line
now has one kneeling person outside the circle*

Representative

In the eternal Commonwealth, the wealth, wit
and wisdom of all people shall be included and
all peoples will walk with their God and with
one another.

All   Amen.

There may be celebration in dance, music or singing

Intercession

The following or other intercessions may follow:

First   God of all people, draw us to the light and be
our guide. In every part of our common life, give
us wise leaders, clear vision and an understanding
of what is right. Inspire in us true values, so
that the wealth and work of each land may be
available to all and for the exploitation of none.

| Second | God bless the head of the Commonwealth, that (s)he may be a sign to us that the different members of our voluntary body may be held together in the service of the common good. |

| Third | May we be a sign to the world of unity in diversity. |

| Fourth | May we work towards a prejudice-free, hate-free, fear-free world. |

| Fifth | May our foreign policy be to earn the trust and gratitude of our neighbours. |

| Sixth | May our mission be 'each according to their ability to each according to their needs'. |

| Seventh | In our lands may employers, employees and shareholders work together like fingers on a hand stretched out for the common good. |

| Eighth | In our sport and leisure may we learn to celebrate with joy, to let a thousand flowers bloom, and to delight in one another's creativity. |

| Ninth | May we know ourselves, know what is good, and know when to stop. |

| Tenth | Give us such a sense of responsibility that, shunning false pride and narrow interests, we may honour one another, seek the common good, and live as fellow citizens of God's kingdom of eternal worth. |

There may be the Lord's Prayer and singing

Leader   God bless the Commonwealth. Make us, your family, mindful of one another, good stewards of your earth, a blessing to the world.

Creative activities

- Display the flag of each Commonwealth country.
- Representatives of Commonwealth countries come in typical national dress.
- Display emblems of each country.
- Perform music, dance or drama from different countries.

Europe

Introduction

Speaking to the European Parliament, former Czech President Vaclav Havel deplored the lack of a moral and spiritual dimension to Europe, and made an appeal for a 'spiritual identity accessible to all citizens'.

The kind of Europe we have will depend upon the motives and goals of those who live in and shape it. If it is just economic, it is not Christian, for money was made for people, not people for money. If it is just political, born out of fear of another war, it will eventually crumble because, as the late Cardinal Basil Hume wrote in his book *Remaking Europe: the Gospel in a Divided Continent*, a Europe born just of economic considerations, or fear of another war, is a negative good, which creates a vacuum which will be filled by the power-hungry.

The fall of Communism has left a vacuum. Europe, without a spiritual vision, could degenerate into nationalist squabbles. The new Europe is a plural society. Deeper, more integrated insights are needed to generate the new dynamic that is needed.

Roman Catholics, Protestants, Orthodox and (especially when Turkey is included) Muslims, as well as floating and non-believers, need to feel it is a spiritual home.

Values that are intrinsic to the European Union include respect for each human life regardless of age, race, or gender; forgiveness for past wrongs; equality of opportunity, equality of treatment under the law; freedom to vote, communicate, travel. These values threaten to be eroded by selfish individualism, pride and prejudice. Green and justice issues have to be addressed.

What is needed is a fellowship across national boundaries of people dedicated to a way of life which bears fruit in these values, people for whom God and good are indivisible.

The Celts are known as the parents of Europe. After they were pushed to the western fringes, they became Christian when the Continent became barbarian. These Celtic Christians then covered Europe again as pilgrims for the love of God, founding communities and cities based on the ideal of laying down one's life for others, forgiveness from the heart for everyone (Rule of St Columba), self-mastery of body and soul. The Celtic churches, like the Orthodox, also believed that a loving relationship with the whole of the natural world is an intrinsic part of holiness.

All this sprang from love of the God of friendship, and commitment to live Christ-like qualities. These Christians were orthodox, and catholic and biblical. We call today's Christians of these now separated traditions to embrace a spirituality which weaves together these strands.

If Mohammed had met Celtic Christians, who understood the Triune God, instead of Arab Christians, who did not, how much would have been different? If Muslims and those of other non-Christian faiths meet Christians with Christ-like qualities, how much will be different? Francis of Assisi's reconciliation visit to the Muslim Sultan reflected this spirituality whereas the Crusades did not.

Each country of Europe has its spiritual wellsprings. Sometimes these have been overlaid. They need to be recovered and used.

As Europe's citizens visit its spiritual wellsprings and draw inspiration from its saints, renewing streams can flow and meet and become a river.

Service of Prayer and Thanksgiving for Europe

All sing   'Sing to God new songs of worship'
Words from Psalm 98, Michael Baughen
Music: Europe's national anthem,
Beethoven's 'Ode to Joy'

Leader   We give thanks that a continent riven by the
worst wars in history now seeks to live in unity.

God's Word

Reader   The prophet envisaged a time when God 'will settle
disputes among the nations, among the great
powers near and far. They will turn their weapons
of war into instruments of blessing, and never
prepare for war again. Everyone will live in peace,
among their own fruitful land, and no one will
make them afraid. The Lord Almighty has
promised this.

Paraphrase of the Prophet Micah 4:3-4

Leader   Our path to peace has developed well,
but many obstacles still confront it.

We give thanks for the glorious and varied
landscapes of our continent, for the rich
produce given us by earth and sea and sky.

All sing   'O Lord my God! when I in awesome wonder
consider all the works thy hand has made'
From a Russian hymn
Words and music: Stuart K. Hine

Leader   We give thanks for the coming to this continent of the civilising Christian Faith. Let us listen to the record of its first mission on our soil, at Macedonia.

Reader   Acts 16:6-15

All sing   'Now thank we all our God'
German hymn by Martin Rinkart,
translated into English by Catherine Winkworth
Music: Johann Crüger

There may be talks, presentations
or the following creative activity

Celebration of saints

Representatives may give thanks for their patron or another national saint. They may do this with national costume, dance, music or visual presentation. A few examples follow

Reader   We give you thanks for Alfred of England,
who made peace with the Danes in Christ's name.
We give thanks for Benedict of Italy, author
of a timeless Rule of Life, co-patron of Europe
We give thanks for Bridget of Sweden,
a peacemaker between nations.
We give thanks for Columbanus of Ireland, who
re-established the faith in many lands of Europe,
and taught us to live as guests of the world.
We give thanks for Cyril and Methodius,
apostles to the Slavs, creators of our language,
co-patrons of Europe.
We thank you for Hildegaard and the Rhineland
mystics, who brought us the vision of love.

105

Reader   We give thanks for Joan of Arc who sought
to make the will of God the will of the people.
We give you thanks for the apostle John,
who fathered loving communities in Turkey.
We thank you for Martin of Hungary
and Tours, who taught us to love the poor.
We give thanks for Nicholas of Switzerland,
father of Swiss democracy.
We give thanks for Seraphim, flame in the snow,
enlightener of Russia.
We give you thanks for Theresa of Spain,
who taught us to renew the inner life.
We give you thanks for Wenceslas of Bohemia,
who taught us the politics of forgiveness.

All sing   'We rest on thee, our shield and our defender'
Words: Edith Gilling of Britain
Music: Finlandia *by Jean Sibelius of Finland*

Intercession

First   May the nations of Europe be freed from the
bondage of fear, rise above selfish ambition,
and become flexible to your direction.

Second   May the qualities that make democracy
function, flourish: homespun qualities
of faithfulness, honesty and care.

Third   Help us never to forget that the blessings of
prosperity and peace come from eternal vigilance
in the struggle against greed, neglect and injustice.

Fourth   Free us from the resentment, mistrust and pride
which divide and confuse our peoples.

Fifth   Give us a heart to serve the poorest peoples
of the world through fair trade and friendly
dealings, and yet to cherish our own minorities
who feel threatened by change.

Sixth   Kindle in us a sense of purpose and a knowledge
that each can make a difference when we are
linked to the Source of all.

Seventh   As we thank you for reconciliation of former
enemies, and the re-uniting of peoples once
divided by an iron curtain, make us instruments
of reconciliation between hostile groups today.

Eighth   As we thank you for the wellsprings of the spirit that
are deep within each nation, we pray that we may
draw from these wells and renew our life today.

Any of the following may be used

Reader   Lord God Almighty,
shaper and ruler of all creatures,
in your mercy guide us to your will,
make our minds steadfast,
strengthen us against temptation,
put injustice far from us.
Shield us against our foes, seen and unseen.
Teach us to inwardly love you before all things
with a clean mind and clean body,
for you are our Maker and redeemer, our trust
and our hope.
                            King Alfred the Great, Britain

Reader   Teach us, good Lord,
          to serve you as you deserve,
          to give and not to count the cost,
          to fight and not to heed the wounds,
          to labour and not to ask for any reward
          except that of knowing that we do your will.

          Ignatius Loyola, Basque, Spain

Reader   Too long have I worried about so many things.
          And yet, my Lord, so few are needed.
          May I today live more simply – like the bread.
          May I today see more clearly – like the water.
          May I today be more selfless – like the Christ.

          From Russia

Reader   My Lord and my God, take from me
          all that keep me from you.
          My Lord and my God, give me all
          that moves me towards you.
          My Lord and my God, take me from myself
          and give me to yourself to own entirely.

          Nicholas of Flue, Switzerland.

Reader   May we know no other love except you
          who are eternal,
          a love so great that the many waters of sky,
          land and sea will fail to quench it.
          Give us, Lord, the love that does not fail;
          renew in us the flame that burns for ever.
          As we continually gaze on you, the Perpetual Light,
          may we shine before you,
          scattering this world's darkness,
          giving light to others.

          Echoes Columbanus, Ireland

Reader   Make us channels of your peace.
Where there is hatred let us bring your love.
Where there is injury, pardon.
Where there is darkness, light.
Where there is despair, hope.
Where there is doubt, faith.
Where there is sadness, joy.
Where there is death, life.
Grant that we may not so much seek
to be consoled as to console,
to be understood as to understand,
to be loved as to love with all our soul.
Francis of Assisi, Italy

Reader   May we be good to others,
as God has been good to us,
and not strive for evil on earth.
From the Koran

All sing   'Thine be the Glory, risen, conquering Son'
*A French hymn by Edmond Budry,
translated into English by R. Birch Hoyle
Music: George Frideric Handel*

Blessing

Leader   May your life be like a flame
that burns through darkest hours,
warming and lighting all who come in
from the cold.

Columbanus

United States of America

Independence Day, 4 July
Thanksgiving, fourth Thursday in November*

Thanksgiving is a national holiday. A festival of this kind was first held by the Pilgrim Fathers who were forcibly exiled from Britain because they wished to worship according to their conscience. They arrived in 1621 and held Thanksgiving in gratitude for a successful harvest after a year of hardship. Subsequently it has become a thanksgiving both for harvest and for God's hand in the history of the USA. Turkey and pumpkin pie are traditionally eaten.

Reader Almighty God,
we thank you for the natural majesty and beauty
of this nation.
They restore us, though we often destroy them.
All Heal us.

Reader We thank you for the great resources
of this nation.
They make us rich, though we often make
others poor.
All Forgive us.

Reader We thank you for the torch of liberty
which has been lit in this land,
and which has drawn people from every nation
to its light.
All Enlighten us.

---

* Canada also has a Thanksgiving Day on the second Monday of October. Some of the above prayers may be used with others from *A Commonwealth Observance.*

Reader	We thank you for the faith we have inherited
	in all its rich variety. It sustains our life,
	though we have often been faithless.
All	Renew us.

Reader	We thank you for the pioneering spirit and hard
	work of those who have made this nation great.
All	Spur us on.

Reader	Help us to know
	that the world does not belong to us,
	that what we do to the world will be done to us.
	May we forego the gods of power and wealth,
	and find our true greatness
	in listening to the world
	and in serving the planet.
All	Humble us.

Reader	Make us wise in our understanding,
	open in our listening,
	generous in our giving
	and vulnerable in our sharing.
All	Lead us.

Service after an Act of Terror

*There may be singing or music and representatives
of the affected area may walk to front seats*

First	In our devastation
All	reach down to us, O God.
Second	In our grief
All	reach down to us, O God.
Third	In our anger
All	reach down to us, O God.
Fourth	In our confusion
All	reach down to us, O God.

Reader   Psalm 7 or another Psalm

There may be singing

Representative 1

I light a candle in memory of . . .

Representative 2

I light a candle in memory of . . .

Representative 3

I light a candle in memory of . . .

There may be a Bible reading and words of comfort

Vigil

*Light candles and sign a condolence book
Place flowers, cards and web messages
Play requiem music*

Teaching

There may be teaching or the following words,
given after the destruction of New York's Twin
Towers on 11 September 2001, may be read – often,
though erroneously, attributed to the Dalai Lama:

Reader　There are two possible responses to what has
occurred today. The first comes from love,
the second from fear . . . Let us not seek
to pinpoint blame, but to pinpoint cause.

We have not learned the most basic human
lessons . . . In short, we have not been listening
to God, and because we have not, we watch
ourselves do ungodly things.

The message we hear from all sources of truth
is clear: we are all one. Forgetting this truth is
the only cause of hatred and war and the way to
remember is simple: love, this and every moment.

Ask God on this day to show us how to show up
in the world in a way that will cause the
world itself to change. And join all the people
in the world who are praying right now, adding
your light to the Light that dispels all fear.

If you wish to experience peace,
provide peace for another.
If you wish to know that you are safe,
cause another to know that they are safe.
If you wish to better understand seemingly
incomprehensible things,
help another to understand.

If you wish to heal your own sadness or anger,
heal the sadness or anger of another.

Intercessions

Reader	Jesus, you were born into a world of oppression.
All	God is with us in oppression.
Reader	Jesus, you were born into a world where the innocent were killed.
All	God is with us when innocent ones are killed.
Reader	Jesus, you were a refugee in Egypt.
All	God is with us when we have to flee.
Reader	Jesus, broken on the Cross,
All	be with the broken in body

Readings Matthew 5:38-48 or Romans 12:9-21

There may be singing

Dedication

A world community of justice

Reader	Bring to birth a community of justice.
All	Help us to understand.
Reader	Have mercy on those who suffer.
All	Help us to understand.
Reader	Help us to weep with those who weep.
All	Help us to understand.
Reader	Help us to heal without festering hate.
All	Help us to understand.
Reader	Have mercy on those who committed these crimes.
All	Help us to understand.

Intercession

Leader	We pray for the powerful who impose their will on the weak.
All	May they come to know your defenceless love.
Leader	We pray for those who seek revenge through acts of terror.
All	May they come to know your defenceless love.
Leader	We pray for those who have lost limbs or loved ones.
All	May they come to know your defenceless love.
Leader	Into your hands we place all that has been.
All	Lord have mercy, Christ have mercy.
Leader	Into your hands we place all that will be.
All	Lord have mercy, Christ have mercy.
Leader	Forgiveness from the heart for everyone.
All	Lord have mercy, Christ have mercy.
Leader	Wounded Christ, touch these wounded souls.
All	Lord have mercy, Christ have mercy.
Leader	Have mercy on all who suffer.
All	Lord have mercy, Christ have mercy.
Leader	Save us and help us in our need.
All	Lord have mercy, Christ have mercy.
Leader	Bring us to eternal light.
All	Lord have mercy, Christ have mercy.
Leader	. . .
All	Lord have mercy, Christ have mercy.
Leader	Glory to the Father, glory to the Son, glory to the Spirit, consoling Three in One.

All   Our Father . . .

Leader   The Tree of Death shall become the Tree of Life.
             The desert shall bloom.
             The trees shall shout.

             Therefore go in the peace
             which Christ alone can give,
             that a hill you shall be in the valley
             and a light you shall be in the dark.

At Public Demonstrations

Public church processions and litanies diminished almost to vanishing point in non-Latin western countries towards the end of the second millennium. They were perceived to be divorced from the heart. At the same time there was an increase in public marches and demonstrations about issues of concern – for example, for the countryside, international debt relief, peace; against global capitalism, racism, tax or price rises.

Christians in earlier centuries, including those in Celtic lands, did not confine their praying to church buildings: their public litanies and processions connected with the concerns of the people. Sometimes a leader would shout a phrase and all the children or adults would shout the same short refrain.

Below we offer four contrasting examples of prayer chants to be used as part of a public demonstration in a world of inter-ethnic hostility. 'All' could refer to all children, all males, all women, etc. Banners, placards and the inclusive Celtic cross may be paraded and the demonstration may be accompanied by music, dancing, giving of food or tokens.

A

Leader	What do we want? We want Muslims.
All	God wants Muslims.
Leader	What do we want? We want Christians.
All	God wants Christians.
Leader	What do we want? We want Jews.
All	God wants Jews.

Leader	What do we want? We want blacks.
All	God wants blacks.
Leader	What do we want? We want whites.
All	God wants whites.
Leader	What do we want? We want browns.
All	God wants browns.
Leader	What do we want? We want justice.
All	God wants justice.
Leader	What do we want? We want peace.
All	God wants peace.
Leader	What do we want? We want love.
All	God wants love.

B

Leader	No prejudice.
All females	God made you, brother.
All males	God made you, sister.

Leader	Jews are Abraham's children.
All females	God made you, brother.
All males	God made you, sister.

Leader	Muslims are Abraham's children.
All females	God made you, brother.
All males	God made you, sister.

Leader	Christians are Abraham's children.
All females	God made you, brother.
All males	God made you, sister.

Leader	All peoples on earth are blessed through Abraham.
All females	God made you, brother.
All males	God made you, sister.

Leader	God cares for the poor.
All females	God made you, brother.
All males	God made you, sister.

Leader	God cares for folk no one else notices.
All females	God made you, brother.
All males	God made you, sister.

Leader	God, forgive us for not caring.
All females	God made you, brother.
All males	God made you, sister.

Leader	Let's do something to change what's wrong.
All females	God made you, brother.
All males	God made you, sister.

C

A large Celtic cross is paraded. The leader points to the circle or cross as indicated by the words. The people repeat *(R)* each phrase after the leader. Phrases can be changed to suit local culture.

Leader	The people are suffering. *(R)* God is suffering. *(R)* The cross is suffering love. *(R)*
Leader	But there's so much despair. *(R)* We feel trapped. *(R)* Trapped inside the circle. *(R)*
Leader	We can't get out. *(R)* Help us, someone. *(R)* It's an endless cycle of doom. *(R)*

Reader   God comes into the circle.
Comes into a baby.
Now he seems one of us.

He gets stuck in the circle.
Betrayed in the circle.
Killed for no reason at all.

The Almighty can't be defeated.
The Almighty raises the dead.
The Almighty breaks through the circle.

He's still with us in the circle.
Now he helps us break through the circle.
Now and for evermore.

Leader   We want to hug everyone. *(R)*
God wants to hug everyone. *(R)*
That's what the circle's about.
All   Amen!

D

Leader	Praise the God of all people.
All	Amen.
Leader	Praise our Father.
All	Amen.
Leader	Praise the Saviour.
All	Amen.
Leader	Praise the Spirit.
All	Amen.
Leader	Praise the God of all people.
All	Amen.

Leader	Praise the All-Compassionate One.
All	Amen.
Leader	Praise the All-Merciful One.
All	Amen.
Leader	Praise the All-Mighty One.
All	Amen.
Leader	. . .
All	Amen.

E

Leader	Creator God,
All	bless the people.
Leader	Saviour God,
All	bless the people.
Leader	Spirit of God,
All	bless the people.

The leader continues to shout the same three phrases, but the cheerleader changes the people's response after each three phrases. Responses such as the following may be used:

. . . bless my neighbour. *(x 3)*
. . . bless my enemy. *(x 3)*
. . . bless our leaders. *(x 3)*

. . . change their hearts. *(x 3)*
. . . change our hearts. *(x 3)*
. . . change everyone's hearts. *(x 3)*

. . . help us. *(x 3)*
. . . guide us. *(x 3)*
. . . trust us. *(x 3)*

SACRAMENTS
AND
SIGNIFICANT
LIFE OCCASIONS

Introduction

The seventh-century *Antiphonary of Bangor* is virtually the only surviving record of Irish church services before they began to be Romanised. *The Stowe Missal*, which came from the monastic church at Tallaght, is the best example we have of an Irish rite which had begun to be Romanised but still retained certain distinctive features. It is a liturgy as celebrated by a Celi De community in ninth-century Ireland.*

We know that a typical church in Celtic Britain had an altar at its centre. Inside a circle of stakes that surrounded the resident members and guests was a wooden church so small that it housed the altar rather than the community. Around was the land the community farmed and the district it accepted into its spiritual care. The Eucharist focused the living heart of Christ reaching out to the life of the district. When the Christians celebrated the Eucharist they were joined to Christ, the Head of the Body of which they were part. They joined their pleadings with those Christ constantly offered to God the Father.

In one place the Eucharist might be celebrated cheerfully, in another sorrowfully, but always with a deep attentiveness. The *Liber Landavensis* claims that the Jerusalem patriarch gave a portable altar to David of Wales, rather than to either of his two colleagues Padarn and Teilo, because he celebrated the Eucharist more cheerfully. Cuthbert of Lindisfarne, on the other hand, used to shed tears from the

---

* Celi De was a spiritual reform movement within the Irish monastic church, meaning 'Clients of God'. The documents known as *The Stowe Missal* are now accessible on the internet and in *Celtic Spirituality* translated by Oliver Davies (Paulist Press, 1999).

depths of his heart when he celebrated the sacrament of 'The Saving Victim'.

There was an awareness that the celebration of the Eucharist was a point of contact between earth and heaven, a focus for divine sustenance and miracle. *Lives* of saints record how the holy celebrants were themselves transformed as they performed the Eucharistic actions. Samson's seventh-century biographer describes how while he was singing the Eucharist, Bishop Dubricius and two monks saw what looked like fire proceeding from his nostrils. 'What is more, the angels of God ever became holy ministers of the altar and of sacrifice along with him.'

Two people told me they heard guitar music during a Holy Communion service at Lindisfarne conducted at 8 o'clock in the morning without music. It seems that angels were more evident than usual.

In the early Church in Celtic lands Holy Communion was celebrated on Sundays, saints' days and special days.

When Earth or Wilderness Eucharists are held it is customary to light a fire whose smoke, according to ancient tradition, cleanses the earth and touches heaven.

The main branches of the Christian Church have their own rites for the sacraments. The material in this volume is not a substitute for these, but an enrichment.

Preparation before Sunday Holy Communion

It is part of Celtic and Orthodox tradition to prepare through prayer on Saturday evening to receive Christ in the liturgy on Sunday morning.

Members of the early churches in Celtic lands truly believed they would feed on Christ himself as they consumed the bread and wine. They recognised that to receive Holy Communion is to receive sustaining food that lasts.

Celtic saints such as Bishop Samson of Dol prepared for Sunday Communion by keeping vigil on Saturday. We know that the tradition of the Columban monasteries, which was carried on by Aidan and Cuthbert in Anglo-Saxon Britain, encouraged Christians to fast from meat and sexual intercourse before receiving Holy Communion.

Celtic Christians were encouraged to examine their conscience and confess their sins. St Patrick taught his followers to pray frequently a form of the Jesus Prayer (Lord, have mercy. Christ, have mercy).

Some may use Saturday evenings to keep silent vigil. Others may choose to repeat slowly the Jesus Prayer for an hour or two: either in its full form (Lord Jesus Christ, truly God, truly human, have mercy upon me a sinner) or in a shorter form.

The personal devotions which we provide here draw upon ancient Celtic litanies, prayers of the Celtic and Eastern Church of the early centuries, and more recent Celtic prayers.

They may be read and repeated slowly in their entirety, or certain prayers may be selected and used in a meditative way.

Section A

O eternal King, the Strengthener, the true and holy Spirit,
you are everywhere and fill all things.
Treasure of blessings, Giver of life,
come and live in us.
Cleanse us from all that is unworthy
of your goodness; save us.

Holy God, Holy and Mighty, Holy and Immortal,
have mercy on us. *(repeat twice more)*

Glory to the Birther,
glory to the Son,
glory to the Holy Spirit,
now and ever to the ages of ages.

Lord, have mercy.
Christ, have mercy.
Lord, have mercy.
(12 times)

O come, let us adore him,
O come, let us adore him,
O come, let us adore him,
Christ the Lord.

He is the King of glory.
He is the King of glory.

He is the King of glory.
Christ the Lord.

For he alone is worthy,
for he alone is worthy,
for he alone is worthy,
Christ the Lord.
(said or sung)

Section B

Psalms 23, 24 or 116:10-16

I know, O Lord,
that I partake unworthily
of your pure and precious body and blood.
I am guilty, and eat and drink condemnation to myself,
not discerning your body and blood,
my Lord and my God.
Yet made bold by your loving kindness I come to you
who said, 'Whoever eats my flesh and drinks my blood
abides in me and I in them.'
So pity me, Lord, and deal with me in mercy.
May these holy things bring me
healing and cleansing, enlightenment and protection,
purifying of soul and body
and diverting of deceptions and the evil workings of the devil.
May these holy things bring me confidence and love
towards you,
change of life and perseverance,
increase of virtue and wholeness,

fulfilment of your requirements,
fellowship with the Holy Spirit,
provision for the journey of life eternal
an acceptable accounting at your fearful judgement seat,
but not judgement or condemnation.

A Prayer of St Basil the Great, d. 379

Lord, grant that my lamp may always be lit,
never extinguished,
that it may always burn and give light to others.
Sweet Saviour, kindle our lamps that they may always shine.
May they always receive Perpetual Light from you
so that the darkness of the world may be scattered.
Give my lamp such a share of your light, my Jesus,
that its brightness may reveal to me the most holy place,
where you, the priest of eternity,
enter the doors of your great dwelling
so that I may always gaze at, adore, and desire only you.
May I love and contemplate you alone.
May my lamp burn and blaze before you for ever.
Most loving Saviour, show yourself to us who seek you,
that, knowing you, we may love you as warmly in return.
May we contemplate you by day and night
and keep you always in our thoughts.
Inspire us with love for you.
May love of you fill all our senses,
a love so great that the many waters of the universe
will fail to quench it.
May this come to us in the gift of our Lord Jesus Christ
to whom be glory for ever and ever. Amen.

From a Prayer of St Columbanus, d. 615

May Mary, and John the youth, and John the Baptist,
and all the Saints of the world
intercede with the fount of true innocence, Jesus Christ,
Son of the Virgin,
that the grace and compassion of the Holy Spirit may come
to forgive us all our past sins,
and to protect us from future sins,
to subdue our fleshly lusts,
and to check our unfitting thoughts.

To kindle the love and affection of the Creator in our hearts
that it may be you that our mind searches after and desires
and meditates on for ever;
that our senses may not be beguiled by trifles;
that you would free our tongues from hollow talk;
that we may not barter the true light and beauty
of everlasting life
for the unrealities of the present life.

May we merit the crown of eternal glory
in the unity of the company of heaven
in the presence of the thrice holy Trinity
through the ages and for ever. Amen.

From an ancient Irish Litany

May Gabriel be with me on Sundays
and the power of the King of heaven.
May Gabriel with me always
that neither evil nor injury may come to me . . .
May the Trinity protect me! May the Trinity defend me!
May the Trinity save me from every hurt, every danger.

An early Irish Prayer to the Archangels

The King of the heavens comes with peace. Alleluia.
Full of the scent of love. Alleluia.
The lovers of your law will never stumble. Alleluia.
The lovers of your law receive your peace. Alleluia.
Oh, sing a song that is new. Alleluia.
Come all you holy ones. Alleluia.
'Eat of my living bread.' Alleluia.
'Drink of the wine I have prepared for you.' Alleluia.

Echoes a Eucharistic Chant in the Stowe Missal

Lord God, I am not worthy that you should come
under the roof of my soul
but as you chose to lie in a cave with dumb animals,
choose to enter the manger of my dumb soul.
And as you did not hold back from entering the house
of Simon the leper
do not hold back from entering the house
of my leprous soul.

Let the purging fire of your most pure Body
and most precious Blood
hallow, enlighten and strengthen my humble soul
and body.
Release me from the burden of my transgressions.
Protect me from the devil.
Take from me harmful habits.
Master my passions.
Increase in me divine grace
and my inheritance in your kingdom.

From Prayers of St John Chrysostom, d. 407

I believe and confess, O Lord,
that you are truly the Christ, Son of the living God,
who came into the world to save sinners
of whom I am first.
I believe this is truly your resurrection body and blood.
Therefore have mercy upon me,
pardon my transgressions, whether committed knowingly
or in ignorance,
that I may partake of your holy Mysteries uncondemned,
for the release from sins and for life eternal.

Admit me to your mystic supper, O Lord.
I will not talk of this to those who are hostile to you
nor give a kiss like Judas, but I will call to you
like the thief:
Remember me, Lord, when you come into your kingdom.
May my sharing in the Holy Mysteries
bring me not condemnation, but healing
of my whole being.

Let us cleanse our consciences from division and contention.
Let our souls be free from hatred and malice to others.
Let us receive holiness, and be inflamed by the Holy Spirit.
Let us receive the Divine Mysteries in unity of mind
and mutual peace
for the resurrection of our bodies, the salvation of our souls
and the life that is everlasting.

From the Malabar Rite –
part of the Syrian and Jacobite tradition
going back to the very early Christian years

Sing praise to God of the Trinity,
excellent unity, divine dwelling.
True praise to the generous Father
and to the Holy Spirit, perfect song.
The outpouring of our splendid praise
sings a song, blood with a word,
to a communion of Three Persons,
of everlasting unity it is made. Amen.

Thirteenth-century Welsh

Section A may be repeated and so on.

Holy Communion

Also called the Eucharist, the Lord's Supper, the Mass and, in early Celtic tradition, Celebration of the Saving Victim

Introduction

Most of the historic branches of the Christian Church offer their own liturgy. The Agreed Statement of all the main branches of the Christian Church, following 50 years' work – *Baptism, Eucharist and Ministry,* published by the World Council of Churches (1982) – declares that in a full celebration of the Lord's Supper the following elements will be present:

- hymns of praise
- penitence and pardon
- proclaiming God's Word
- confessing the Faith
- intercession
- preparing bread and wine
- thanking God for creating, saving and purifying us
- repeating Christ's words when instituting the Supper
- remembering Christ's birth, passion death, rising from death, ascension and Pentecost
- inviting the Holy Spirit on the faith community and/or the bread and wine
- the congregation offering itself to God
- a sign of reconciliation (peace)
- breaking of bread

- eating and drinking in unity with Christ and one another
- blessing and sending

The following Order provides material for each of these elements. It may be used as it is, or sections may be woven in to the existing patterns of Eucharist of any branch of the Church.

The gathering

This may take many forms, from informal gatherings in homes or large venues to singing and praying before a church service or the Liturgy. It is not essential that the ordained person who presides at Holy Communion is present during the gathering.

There may be music making, dancing and singing
The following song may be sung:

All sing   Gather around for the table is spread.
Welcome the food and rest!
Wide is our circle, with Christ at the head,
he is the honoured guest.
Learn of his love, grow in his grace,
pray for the peace he gives;
here at this meal, here in this place,
know that his Spirit lives!
Once he was known in the breaking of bread,
shared with a chosen few;
multitudes gathered and by him were fed;
so he will feed us too.

Tune: Skye boat song*

---

* Words by Jean Holloway. © 1994, 1999 Kevin Mayhew Ltd

Leader	Let us make room in our hearts to welcome Christ in one another.
All	Christ is in you, Christ is in me.
Leader	Let us welcome Christ in friend or stranger at the door.
All	Christ is in them, Christ is in us.

Either

Reader	We would prepare a feast and be host to the great High King, with all the company of heaven. We would offer the roots of repentance, baskets of love, cups of mercy for the company. Sweet Jesus, be with us, with all the company of heaven. May cheerfulness abound as we feast with the great High King, our host for all eternity.

or

Leader	Jesus said: Where two or three are gathered together in my name, I am there in their midst.
All	Christ is present with us now.

or

Leader	Let this wondrous creation, plundered by alien forces, open wide its arms to its returning Saviour. Let all the people, marked with the Creator's dignity, welcome him who comes to restore our lost innocence.
All	As the birds brought food to your people in the parched deserts, so now you bring food to our parched and hungry souls.

or

Leader Open our eyes to you, tender Lamb of eternity,
Blessed Sacrament of self-giving.
Help us to enter into your life outpouring.

Penitence and pardon

Reader Grant me tears, O Creator,
flowing in streams from my eyes.
In pools from my inmost parts bring forth tears.

Old Irish

Leader As we draw near to the place of at-one-ment:
give us tears to see the wonder of your presence;
give us tears to see the wasting of your people;
give us tears to see the wounding of your Son.

*Anyone may speak out hurts, pains or sorrows with
which they or the world around is oppressed*

Leader
All All holy, all-merciful God,
we are the race that helped cut the wood
on which you were crucified,
and still we misuse your creation;
we are the race that helped make the nails
that pierced your body,
yet still we use work for gain at others' expense;
we are the race that did nothing
to stop your betrayers,
yet still we are ruled by comfort or cowardice.

or all sing

Lord, have mercy. *(x 8)*
Christ, have mercy. *(x 8)*
Lord, have mercy. *(x 8)*

or

All   God, make us holy.
Christ, make us holy.
In the name of the Spirit holy,
God, the Three all-holy,
we confess our sins to you,
Father, Son and Spirit holy.
Compassionate God of life,
your kindly pardon give:
for our careless talk,
our broken promises,
our empty speech,
for all that we have left undone,
for all that we have done amiss.

Leader   Jesus, tender Lamb of the tears and the piercings,
as we receive your forgiveness
enshield us, encircle us each day, each night.
Uphold us, be our treasure,
our triumph everlasting,
strong Son of our God most high.

or

Leader   O souls, be joyful;
the saving God stretches out his hand to you
to announce a loving reconciliation.
Washed and made whole,
let us listen to the Word of Christ.

God's Word

Reader	Let us attend, the sharp-edged sword of the Word of God comes to us.
All	Thanks be to God.
Reader	Illumine our hearts, O Lord, implant in us a desire for your truth; may all that is false within us flee.

Reader   *The Old Testament reading for the day*

There may be singing

Reader   *The Gospel reading for the day*

There may be singing, silence, teaching, creative activities, or sharing of words from God

Declaring the Faith

This 'Creed of St Patrick' may be declared by all or by three voices as indicated:

First   Our God is the God of all humans,
the God of heaven and earth,
the God of seas and rivers,
the God of the sun and moon,
the God of the stars and planets,
the God of the lofty mountains,
the God of the lowly valleys.

Second   God is above the heavens and is beneath
the heavens.
Heaven and earth and sea and everything
that is in them are God's abode.

God inspires all things, gives life to all things,
stands above all things.
God is the light-giver of the sun, the night
and the stars.
It is God who makes wells in arid land
and islands in the sea,
who places the stars in service of the galaxies.

Third God has a Son who is co-eternal
and similar with himself;
the Son is not younger than the Father,
nor the Father older than the Son,
and the Holy Spirit breathes in them.
And the Father and the Son and the Holy Spirit
are inseparable.

All Amen.

or

Leader We believe, O God of all gods,
that you are the eternal Maker of life.
We believe, O God of all gods,
that you are the eternal Maker of love.

All We believe, O Lord and God of all people,
that you are the Creator of the high heavens,
that you are the Creator of the skies above,
that you are the Creator of the oceans below.

Leader We believe, O Lord and God of all people,
that you are the One who created our souls
and set their course,
that you are the One who created our bodies
from earth,
that you gave to our bodies their breath
and to our souls their possession.

All   God, bless to us our bodies.
God, bless to us our souls.
God, bless to us our living.
God, bless to us our goals.

Intercession

These may include any of the following:

Leader   Grant, O Lord,
that your church in this land may be true
to its birthright.
Kindle in us the adventure of obedience, the single
eye, the humble, generous spirit which marked
Aidan, Hilda and your Celtic saints.

As we will bring this bread to you,
so we offer you the sap of life rising;
our energies and all that we create;
the fun, the relationships,
and the communications of life.

As we will pour out wine,
so we offer to you
the woes of life outpouring;
the waning powers, disease and disappointments;
hurts and handicaps.

As grapes are crushed to make the wine,
so we offer to you all who are crushed
by hunger or homelessness, violence or abuse.

The leader or any may mention examples

You who put beam in sun and moon,
take all this, and transform it
into the deep, rich wine of everlasting life.

A sign of reconciliation

Leader   Peace with yourself.
Peace with creation.
Peace with one another.
The peace of Christ be with you.

All   The peace of Christ be with you.

Leader   Let us greet one another with these words.

or

Leader   In this feast comes the root of our joy;
in this feast Christ comes:
 the King of greatness.
Let us prepare for him by giving one another
a sign of his peace.
The peace of the Lord be always with you.

All   And also with you.

or

Leader   Peace with the land and all that grows on it.
Peace with the sea and all that swims in it.
Peace with the air and all that flies through it.
Peace with your God who calls you to serve.

or

Leader	Let us make room in our hearts
	to welcome Christ in one another.
All	Christ is in you, Christ is in me.
Leader	Let us welcome Christ in friend
	or stranger at the door.
All	Christ is in them, Christ is in us.

Dedication of the faith community

Leader   At the last supper Jesus shared his journey
and asked his disciples to become one with
him. Through bread and wine we renew our
communion with earth and we acknowledge our
interwovenness with the broken ones of the world.

All   Risen Christ, we welcome you.
You are the flowering bough of creation;
from you cascades music like a million stars,
truth to cleanse a myriad souls.
From you flee demons, omens and all ill will;
around you rejoice the angels of light.
Father, send us the tender Spirit of the Lamb;
feed us with the Bread of heaven;
may we become drunk with your holiness.

Where gifts of the people are offered up:

Leader   Remember, O Lord,
those who have made you this offering,
and those for whom it is offered.
Accept the gifts of your servants, whether much
or little, given in secret or openly,
and of those who wish to give
but have nothing with which to give.

Accept their ready mind,
and fill their household with good things
and as they remember your holy name on earth.
Remember them in your heavenly kingdom,
and in this world do not forsake them for ever.

Ethiopian Orthodox liturgy

Leader   Now let us lay aside all cares of this life
that we, like the angels,
may offer you our worship,
joining with them in singing to the thrice holy,
and life-giving Trinity:

All sing or say

All   Holy, holy, holy is the Lord,
holy is the Lord God almighty! *(x 2)*
Who was, and is, and is to come!
Holy, holy, holy is the Lord!

Glory . . .

Preparing bread and wine

Either

Leader   We bless you, King of all creation.
Through your goodness we have this bread and
wine to offer,
which earth has given and human hands have
made;
they will become our spiritual food and drink.

or

Leader   As the grain once scattered on the fields
and the grapes once dispersed upon the hillside
are now reunited on this table in bread and wine;
so, Lord, may your whole church soon be gathered
from earth's four corners to be one at the feast
in your coming kingdom.

Recalling Christ's institution of the Lord's Supper

*In many liturgies this forms a section of the
Thanksgiving Prayer*

Leader   Among friends, gathered round a table,
Jesus took bread, broke it, and said,
'This is my body – broken for you.'
Later he took a cup of wine and said,
'This is the new relationship with God
made possible because of my death.
Take it, all of you, to remember me.'

or

Leader   On the night he was betrayed Jesus took bread,
gave you thanks, broke it *(the president may
break bread in to two halves)* and gave it *(the
president may stretch out both arms with one half
of the bread in each hand, to signify Christ's arms
stretched out on the cross embracing all people in
love)* to his disciples saying: 'Take, eat, this is
my body which is given for you.' After supper
he took the cup *(the president holds up the cup or
chalice)*, gave you thanks, and said to them:

'Drink, all of you; this is my blood
of the new covenant which is shed for you
and for many for the forgiveness of sins.
Do this in remembrance of me.'

Thanksgiving

*In many liturgies the recalling of Christ's redeeming
life, passion, death, resurrection, ascension – and of
Pentecost and the birth of the Christian Church –
is included in the Thanksgiving Prayer*

A

Leader Lift up your hearts.
All We lift them to the Lord.
Leader Let us offer thanks for all God has done.
All You lead your people through the years.
Leader High King of the universe, you brought forth the
earth; you breathe wisdom into all your creatures,
till we reflect your Three-fold friendship.

Father, all powerful and ever-living God,
we do well always and everywhere to give you
thanks through Jesus Christ our Lord.
You, O Father, with your only Son
and the Holy Spirit are God.
You are God, one and immortal;
God, incorruptible and unmoving;
God, invisible and faithful;
God, wonderful and worthy of praise;
God, strong and worthy of honour;
God, most high and magnificent;
God, living and true;

God, wise and powerful;
God, holy and splendid;
God, great and good;
God, awesome and peace-loving;
God, beautiful and righteous;
God, pure and kind;
God, blessed and just;
God, tender and holy.

You are God, not in the singularity of one
person, but in the trinity of one substance.

We believe in you;
we bless you;
we adore you;
and we praise your name for evermore.

We praise you through Christ
who is the salvation of the universe;
through Christ who is the life of human beings;
through Christ who is the resurrection of the dead.

Through him the angels praise your majesty;
the dominations adore;
the powers of the heavens tremble;
so may we join with them in saying:

All   Holy, Holy, Holy Lord,
God of power and might,
heaven and earth are full of your glory.
Hosanna in the highest.

From the Stowe Missal

B

Leader   Living God, we acclaim you, majestic in holiness,
worthy of praise, worker of wonders.
In the beginning you created the universe.
You made the sun and stars above our heads,
the earth beneath our feet.
Your word brought forth the rocks and streams,
the surging seas, the wild animals and birds.

You fashioned life in all its myriad forms,
and shaped from clay
the wonder of the human frame.

You spoke your word to those you had chosen;
in disobedience they turned from your commands.
You came to them yourself in Christ,
the Word made flesh;
but he was shamed, despised by all;
forsaken in the darkness of the Cross.

You made the Tree of Death the Tree of Life,
the empty grave a sign of glorious hope.
You raised your Son
and brought him to your side again,
where now he lives; to pray on our behalf.
Therefore with all your people,
and with the whole company of heaven,
we praise you in the angels' hymn:

All   Holy, holy, holy, Lord,
God of power and might,
heaven and earth are full of your glory.
Hosanna in the highest.

C

Leader	The Lord be with you.
All	And also with you.
Leader	Lift up your hearts.
All	We lift them to the Lord.

| Leader | Let us give thanks to the Lord our God. |
| **All** | It is right to give our thanks and praise. |

Leader It is indeed right, for you made us,
and, before us, you made the world we inhabit,
and, before the world,
you made the eternal home in which,
through Christ, we have a place.

The vast cosmos and the tiny seed have their
origin in you; all that is lovely, all who are
loving, point to you as their fulfilment.

And grateful as we are for the world we know
and the universe beyond our ken,
we above all praise you,
whom eternity cannot contain,
for coming to earth and entering time in Jesus.

For his life which informs the way we live,
for his compassion which changes our hearts,
for his plain truths which show up
our trivial chatter,
for his disturbing presence,
his innocent suffering, his fearless dying,
his rising to life, breathing forgiveness,
we praise and worship you.

Leader	We thank you for the Holy Spirit,
	who confronts us with your claims
	and attracts us to your goodness.
	Therefore we gladly join our voices to the song
	of your people on earth and in heaven:

All	Holy, Holy, Holy Lord,
	God of power and might,
	heaven and earth are full of your glory.
	Hosanna in the highest.

Leader	And now, setting our wisdom, our will,
	our words aside,
	emptying our hearts, and bringing nothing
	in our hands,
	we yearn for the healing, the holding,
	the accepting, the forgiving
	which Christ alone can offer.

D

The creator of all flesh lived in the womb:
he who forms infants in the womb
became an infant;
they wrapped in swaddling cloths
him who was clothed with light.
He dwelt in the house of the poor as poor.
He walked as a man, yet worked as God.
Willingly he became hungry
as a child of humanity,
and, multiplying a little bread
satisfied the hunger of many.

He thirsted as a dying man,
and changed water into wine
as the one who is able to give life to all.
He slept as the children of the flesh,
and awoke and rebuked the winds as a creator.
He became tired and rested as the humble
and walked upon the water as the highest.
He, before whom the angels bow their heads
in awe,
bowed his head before the crucifiers to suffer.
A weak tree carried him
who carries both heaven and earth.
He died to destroy death.
He died to give life to the dead,
to gather together those who were scattered,
and turn sinners to glory and honour.

Ethiopian Orthodox liturgy

Reader   Alas, we have seen the Son of the living God
stretched out on a cross;
alas, the body that possesses wisest dignity
has been plunged into blood;
a crown of thorns placed about his beauteous head.
The blood of Christ is flowing
through his gleaming sides.
This cross is like the parting of the day from night.
Yet through it, all may now proclaim:

All   Christ has died!
Christ is risen!
Christ will come again!

Inviting the Holy Spirit

Leader Holy Spirit,
as we partake of this bread and this wine,
may we re-member the Body of Christ.

or

By the power of your Holy Spirit
may these gifts of bread and wine
be for us Christ's body and blood.

or

Living God,
change these elements of bread and wine
and the elements of our lives
with the transforming power of your presence,
that this communion may become a foretaste
of your new creation.

or

Bless these gifts of bread and wine
with the dew of your Spirit.

*In the Irish language edition of the Roman
Catholic Eucharistic Prayer 11*

or

Merciful God,
send now, in kindness, your Holy Spirit
to settle on this bread and wine and fill them
with the fullness of Jesus.
And let that same Spirit rest on us, converting us
from the patterns of this passing world,
until we conform to the shape of him
whose food we now share.

The invitation to receive

Leader   Christ invited to his feast all for whom he died.

The world's churches in Baptism,
Eucharist and Ministry

or

Leader   He whom the universe could not contain,
is present to us in this bread.
He who redeemed us and called us by name
now meets us in this cup.
So take this bread and this wine.
In them God comes to us
that we may come to God.

Stowe Missal

or

Leader   This is the table of Christ,
our host through all eternity.
So come, you who feel weak and unworthy,
you who come often
and you who have stayed away.
Come, you who love him
and you who wish you could.
Come, you who are hungry
for friendship or forgiveness.
Come, you who long for meaning or a just world.

Echoes a prayer of the Iona Community

or

Leader   This is a table to feed the starving poor,
a table to strengthen the weak.

Here we may touch the broken body of Jesus.
Here our hearts melt like wax before a fire.

Echoes a Welsh hymn of Morris Williams
(1809-1874)

or

Leader   All-Compassionate, All-Embracing One,
you invite to your table people from the East
and people from the West,
Jew and Arab, male and female, young and old.
You invite to your table rich and poor.
You invite to your table ancient peoples
and new peoples, black, brown and white.

Eating, drinking and communing with Christ

Communicant

This precious nectar is my delight.
From this cup flows warmth for my darkest night,
from you I drink in poise and power,
though I am broken, in a needy hour.
And cup-sharing with me are rich and poor;
folk of all kinds all thirsty for more.

Any of the following words from the Stowe Missal
may be read; for use during the distribution

Readers   My peace I give to you,
my peace I leave with you, Alleluia.

John 14:27

The lovers of your law have great peace,
they never stumble, Alleluia.

Psalm 119:165

The King of heaven comes with peace,
full of the scent of love, Alleluia.

Come, all my holy ones, eat of my bread,
drink of the wine I have made for you, Alleluia.

Whoever eats my body and drinks my blood
lives in me and I in them.

John 6:56

Come, you who are loved by my Father,
inherit the kingdom prepared for you
before the foundation of the world, Alleluia.

Matthew 25:34

*All may sing the following to the tune of
The Skye Boat Song*

All sing Many the grains from fields near and far
now on this table as one.
Many from places afar are now here
in one communion.

One body, one bread,
one Lord of all,
one cup which blesses all.
And we though many
throughout the world
bring healing to the earth.

Repeat first verse

Final act of praise or prayer

Leader   Heaven is intertwined with earth.
All   Alleluia!
Leader   We have taken the divine life into ourselves.
All   Alleluia!

or

Leader   When your blood was spilled on the soil,
earth was transformed
and the Tree of Death became the Tree of Life.
Through this Eucharist may we be instruments
of your transforming love.

All   As we share this foretaste of the heavenly feast,
generous be our hearts,
open be our hands,
justice be our benchmark,
thanksgiving be our call.

or

Leader   Encircle with your care the world
and all her people.
Support those who govern us
and those who seek the good of others.
At your table there is no despising:
Easterner and Westerner, rich and poor
join hands with you.
So send us out to build a world
free from prejudice, hate and fear.

or

All When our way is weary
we will look to you, our Providence,
to come with strengthening angels.

When our frames are hungry
we will look to you, our Providence,
to come with food for our hearts.

or

Leader Grant, Lord, that the ears which have heard
the voice of your songs
may never listen to the voice of clamour
and discord;
that the tongues which have sung
'Holy, holy, holy' may speak the truth;
and the bodies which have tasted
your living Body
may be restored to newness of life.
Let your great love remain with us.

From the Malabar Rite –
part of the Syrian and Jacobite tradition
going back to the very early Christian years.

Sending and blessing

Leader And so now each may say:
All We rise up clothed in strength of Christ.

First We shall not be imprisoned.
Second We shall not be harmed.
First We shall not be down-trodden.

Second	We shall not be left alone.
First	We shall not be tainted.
Second	We shall not be overwhelmed.
All	We go clothed in Christ's white garments.
	We go freed to weave Christ's patterns.
	We go loved to serve Christ's weak ones.
Leader	Go in peace to love and serve the Lord.
All	In the name of Christ. Amen.

Sharing blessed bread with everyone

*An assistant holds a large basket of freshly baked bread
cut into small chunks and offers these to everyone.
There may be refreshments and feasting*

This custom of sharing blessed bread, which was practised in
the Celtic Church, is needed in today's churches as long as
certain sections of the church withhold the consecrated bread
and wine from members of other sections of the church.

A 'St Cuthbert Holy Communion'

*The following material may be used within the
framework of a faith community's usual Eucharist*

The Celtic Alleluia may be sung

Preparation for confession

Leader   When Cuthbert offered up the Saving Victim as
a sacrifice to God, he offered his prayer to the
Lord not by raising his voice but by shedding
tears which sprang from the depths of his heart.

Bede

Reader   When the soul grows tearful, weeps, and is filled
with tenderness, and all this without having
striven for it, then let us run, for the Lord has
arrived uninvited and is holding out to us the
sponge of loving sorrow . . . these tears have a
power greater than anything that comes from
our own thoughts and our own meditation.

*John Climacus, Abbot of Sinai,
seventh century*

Silence; forgiveness is declared

God's Word

Reader   God brought food to his hungry people in the
desert. Let us recall how he brought food to his
servant Elijah:
1 Kings 17:1-6

Reader   Let us recall how God also brought food
to folk in Cuthbert's time:

Cuthbert was travelling south along the river
Teviot, teaching and baptising the country folk
in the hill areas. He had a boy with him, whom
he sought to train in an understanding of God's
providence. 'Do you think anyone has prepared
your midday meal today?' he asked the boy. The
boy said he knew of no friends or relatives on
their route so he did not expect provision
from anyone. 'Don't worry, but seek first the
kingdom of God and the Lord will provide for
all your needs,' Cuthbert told him. 'I have been
young; now I am old, but I have never seen God
forsake those who do what is right.'

Some time later Cuthbert saw an eagle in the
sky and said: 'This is the eagle which the Lord
has instructed to provide us with food today'.
Shortly, the eagle settled on the river bank, and,
at Cuthbert's bidding, the boy walked over to it
and took away a large fish which the eagle had
brought. Cuthbert said, 'Why did you not leave
half of this for our fisherman to eat?' The boy
returned half the fish to the eagle, they broiled
their half of the fish in the company of some men
who had a fire going, and shared their fish with
them, too. They thanked the Lord, worshipped
him, and went on their way to the hill people.

Leader   As the birds brought food to your people in the
parched deserts, and to your people in Celtic
lands, so you will bring food to our parched
and hungry souls.

Leader	God who put ear in corn and cattle,
All	you are the Rock from which all earth is fashioned.
	You are the Food from which all souls are fed.

Thanksgiving

Leader	Let us recall blessings of Providence to us
	in recent days and name them aloud or in silence:
Any	*(name blessings)*

There may be singing

Reader Matthew 18:12-14

and

Cuthbert trudged through plague-devastated villages to minister to the few poor people who remained. He was about to leave one village when he asked the priest, 'Are you sure there is no one left whom I have not seen?' The priest looked around, and found one tear-stained woman standing at a distance. She had lost one son in the plague, and now seemed about to lose her other son, whom she was holding in her arms. Cuthbert made his way to her, blessed her, kissed the boy, and said to his mother, 'There is no need to be sad any more. Your infant will be healed and will live, and no one else in your family will die from this plague.'

Intercession

Leader   Tender Father, who called Cuthbert from tending sheep to be a shepherd of the people; help us, inspired by his example, to heal the sick, guard unity, storm heaven's gates, and bring those who are lost home to your fold, through Jesus Christ our Lord.

Leader   Cuthbert had a care for the Church and guarded its unity, its holiness and its heart for mission. Let us have a time of prayer for the Church and its mission.

Sign of reconciliation

Leader   Cuthbert's last words were 'Always keep God's peace and love among you'.
The peace of the Lord be always with you.
All   And also with you.

Holy Communion

This now takes place. Material in preceding pages may be used.

Deep Re-membering
Eucharist for Healing the Land

A 'Healing the Land' Eucharist needs to be prepared by representatives of a whole community following a period of study, prayer and discernment of the communal roots that need healing.

An agreed list is drawn up of who has been dismembered over the years in the local community. Groups that have been fragmented, embittered, and in that sense dismembered from the whole should be included.

A second task is to listen deeply to and draw out through dialogue the longings and convictions of those who feel themselves, for whatever reason, to be dismembered.

During the preparation season it is important to explain that both the failures and the hopes of everyone are, as it were, to be brought together and placed in Christ's chalice at the forthcoming special Holy Communion service.

At this service different representatives can tell the story, as they see it, without blame, in words or pictures.

There may be a Disarming Ritual. A representative kneels before a symbol of oppression of the group (for example, a potato could be used as a symbol of the Irish potato famine). A representative of the other side brings a gift or makes some other act of restitution.

A large chalice such as a silver bowl is placed on the table or altar. Each representative places the record of what they have told (in writing or picture) in the chalice.

During the Holy Communion service these are placed alongside the bread and wine, and the person presiding says this prayer:

Gracious Father,
take the sufferings and wounded memories
of these your children into the heart of Christ,
who fills all and is in all.

Healing Christ,
take the hopes and aspirations
of these your children into your heart,
that they may be purified and come to fulfilment.

Holy Spirit,
pour upon these elements of bread and wine,
and upon these elements of our wounds and hopes,
and transform them.

Great God of the human family,
the Three of Limitless Love,
as we share together in this Holy Communion,
may we re-member the Body of Christ.

Eucharist of the Holy Grail

This is an experimental pattern of worship which uses the myth of the grail as an imaginative vehicle to throw light on aspects of the observance of the historical Last Supper of Christ. It is adapted from the original version by Richard Deimel.

Invocation

Leader   We call upon Gabriel,
healer of the wounded,
messenger of the Light of God,
Archangel of the Chalice,
and here with us now.

All   Protect us in the name of Christ,
with the mighty sword of his Spirit,
the true sword of our land.

Confession

Leader   We your people confess that in our rich world many are bound by hunger.

All   Sword of the Almighty, break their chains.

Leader   We your people confess that in our beautiful world much of created life is being killed by our pollution.

All   Celtic holy men and women, show us how to clean the land.

Leader   We your people confess that in our peaceful world all created life is seconds away from nuclear holocaust.

All   God of the Holy Grail, give us a power to destroy
               false power.

Leader   O God who gave birth to the universe,
               lead us to the beauty of your Grail
               and be born again in our lives.

The Round Table – exploring the vision

Reader   Psalm 72; John 19:33-37 or Revelation 21:1-7

Storyteller *The story of King Arthur and his Knights by Sir
               Thomas Malory, derived from chapter 17 (20), may
               be told or read by a single reader or with a second
               reader for the part of Christ (JC) as follows:*

It seemed to them that there came an old man
and four angels from heaven, clothed in the likeness of a bishop and with a cross in his hand.
And these four angels bore him up in a chair and
set him down before the table of silver where the
Holy Grail was. And it seemed that he had on
his forehead letters which said:

See you here Joseph, the first Bishop of
Christendom, the same who our Lord succoured
in the City of Sarras in the spiritual palace.

They heard the chamber door open and there
they saw angels. And two held candles of wax
and the third held a towel and the fourth a spear
which bled marvellously, so the drops fell into a
box which he held with his other hand. And
they set the candles upon the table and the third
the towel upon the vessel and the fourth the holy
spear upright on the vessel.

The Bishop took bread. As he lifted the bread there came a figure like a child. Then he lifted the vessel of the Holy Grail. 'Now,' he said, 'the servants of Jesus Christ, you shall be fed at this table with sweetmeats that knights never tasted.' And he vanished away.

They sat down at the table in great dread and prayed. Then they looked and saw a man come out of the holy vessel who bore all the wounds of Jesus Christ bleeding openly and said:

JC   My knights and my servants and my true children, who have come out of deadly life into the spiritual life, you shall now see a part of my hidden secrets. Now hold and receive the High Order and meet that which you have so much desired.

Minister Then he took the holy vessel and came to Sir Galahad. And he kneeled down and received his Saviour. And after him so received all his comrades. And they thought it so sweet that it was marvellous to tell. Then he said to Sir Galahad:

JC   Son, do you know what I hold in my hands? This is the Holy Grail from my Last Supper, which you so longed to see. Now you must go from here and bear with you this holy vessel, for this night it must leave this land. And do you know why? Because the Spirit is not rightly served and worshipped by them of this land, for they have turned to evil living.

There follows a sharing of the vision
How is the Spirit, supremely manifested
in the total self-giving of Christ in the Last Supper,
best served and worshipped by us?

This could be a Round Table sharing,
if numbers are not too great

Declaration of belief

All   In God
there is no female or male,
no past, present and future,
no living and dead,
no black and white,
no failure and success.
In God
there is only
light and love
to all and in all and for all for ever.

Making ready

There may be singing while bread and wine
and the symbols are made ready

If a gift-offering is taken, when this is offered
we raise our hands to the offering and say:

All   Holy One,
you are our only Treasure,
you are our Heart's Desire.
Now we give you the best we have.
Take us and use us for your highest purposes.

The breaking of the bread
and the sharing of the chalice

Males   *(while one female holds in focus a piece of rock)*
God of Earth,
you are the Rock that all the glory of mountain,
wood and field is built on.

Females   *(while one male holds in focus a large jug and
basin and pours water)*
God of Water,
you fill the cup with the stream of life
to bring birth and beauty and blessing.

Males   *(while one female holds in focus a metal bowl of
burning charcoal, to be used later for incense)*
God of Fire,
you fill the cauldron of life
with blazing energy of cosmic atom
to bring sun and work and change.

Females   *(while one male waves in focus a coloured flag, as
big as possible)*
God of Air,
you lift us into new dimensions out of our bodies
through the skies
into time beyond millennium time.

All   *(while all symbols are held in focus together)*
O God of Earth, Water, Fire and Air,
we praise you with tongue and drum and guitar:
Hosanna in the highest . . .

There is singing and music

Female   People turned away from God.
They used the elements of the cosmos
for power and pain.
History tells of Christ coming as Champion
of the world through his body broken on the cross
and his grave broken by the power
of his risen body.

Male   Stories tell of Arthur winning battles to save
Britain from returning darkness.
Columba, Aidan, Cuthbert all brought dazzling
light to heal the land.
Brigid and Hilda brought fire which burns for ever.

All   Come, Holy Spirit, to our nation.
Make this a new Age of Love in our land.

Minister   Grant that by the power of your Holy Spirit
these gifts of bread and wine
may be to us Christ's body and his blood.
At his Last Supper,
Jesus took bread and gave you thanks;
he broke it and gave it to his disciples, saying:
Take, eat; this is my body which is given for you;
do this in remembrance of me.
Now we give thanks for this pure
and sweet-smelling loaf,
the Waybread for our journey home
to the unknown world.

Male   An old story walks our land again.
Holy people of long ago told of a Green Chapel,
a small, stone prayer house deep in the old forest
in the shadow of ancient trees.

Outside wild birds sing a sweet song
while a small stream trickles on stone.
Inside a deep green light
pours on to a rough stone altar.
On the altar there is a cup, the Cup of Christ's
blood dazzling with rainbow light.
Anyone who looks on the Cup
is healed of all hurt.

The Cup is raised high

Holy Spirit, raise up the Cup of the Grail
high over our nation
to heal sick minds and broken families
and lead us into a New Age.

Minister Because after his Last Supper Jesus took that cup
in his holy work-stained hands
and gave you thanks; he gave it to them, saying:
Drink this, all of you;
this is my blood of the new age,
which is shed for you and for many
for the forgiveness of evil, so death may be healed.
Do this, as often as you drink it,
in remembrance of me.
Now we give thanks for this Grail Chalice,
blood from the wounded Fisher King Jesus,
desire of all our hearts.

All Christ has died,
Christ is risen,
Christ will come again!

Incense is placed on the burning charcoal
All sing a hymn such as 'Restore O Lord', while two
children hold the loaf and cup

We share the loaf and cup, in a circle, while gentle
music is played

Healing prayer may be offered

Leader Holy Spirit,
All you have found us today in your broken
and healing bread and in your Cup of love.
May we seek your Grail every morning,
work in your power every day
and rejoice in your mellow love every night.

There may be singing and celebration

Agape Meal

An Agape is an informal meal during which bread and drink are shared as symbols of fellowship with God and with one another. Agape is the Greek word for love as unconditional self-giving.

The Agape was popular with the first Christians, who broke bread from house to house (Acts 2:46, 20:7; Jude 12). For a short period the fellowship meal was combined with the memorial of Christ's death ('the Lord's Supper' or Eucharist) but this was abused and therefore devalued the Lord's Supper (see 1 Corinthians 11:17-34), so it was discontinued. In recent times, however, a feeling has grown that the Eucharist has become too formalised and disconnected from some of its original aspects; that there is a need for relaxed, informal fellowship to come to the fore. Hence the rise of the Agape.

In the historic churches an Agape differs from a Eucharist in these ways: The person who presides need not be ordained; the drink need not be wine; the bread and wine are not used as symbols of Christ's death; and the words of Christ instituting the Last Supper are not used.

Although the bread and drink in an Agape should be used as symbols of God's gifts of creation and human fellowship, and not specifically of Christ's death, the Agape nevertheless echoes other aspects of the last supper that Jesus shared with his disciples. An important part of this meal is an extended grace, with Jewish roots, which includes the blessing of the loaf and some grape juice or wine. As a shared meal the Agape also draws out elements in the original Christian Eucharist which, in some parts of the Church, have been overlooked. It reminds us that the

Eucharist is a meal made up of ordinary food and drink, the basic bread and wine of human life. It includes the offering to God of the created gifts of life.

Food represents the fundamental stuff of life and its goodness. We take this world into ourselves each time we eat; we change the food into ourselves and it becomes energy in us. God's purpose for food is that it gives us physical life so that we might relate directly to the Source who gave us life and who pours out his life. So the eating of the food, in this way of thinking, becomes life-giving. It restores thanksgiving to the human race.

An Agape may be held at any time, but in the contemporary Celtic renewal Thursday evening (Jesus' last supper was on a Thursday) and Friday evening (reflecting the Jewish practice of a meal on the eve of the Sabbath) are the days when the Agape is most frequently observed.

If it takes place outdoors a fire may be lit.

Leader You are here in this place, Lord.
All Your Spirit is with us.

Reader Who are we? What are we here for?
All We are here as mortals made in God's likeness,
enjoying the One who nurtures our being,
returning all life back to God with praise.

There may be singing and merry making

Leader Good God, our host through all eternity,
gathered here we rejoice that your Spirit permeates
all creation, inspiring your earth to bring forth
food and drink, energy and life, that we may
now offer this back to you, who gives us all.

All   Glory to you, our Creator;
glory to you, our Friend;
glory to you, Spirit who breathes life into all.

Leader   This meal becomes a parable of how all created
life is meant to be:

All   Offered, blessed, enjoyed in communion
with God and with one another.

Leader   This meal is a foretaste of our final destiny
which is pictured as a banquet of the human
family with its God.

Reader   *Revelation 19:5-9 or the following:*
Jesus said, 'I assure you that many will come
from the east and the west and sit down with
Abraham, Isaac, and Jacob at the feast in the
kingdom of heaven.'

                                       Matthew 8:11

    The host lights a table candle

Host   I would prepare a feast and be host to the great
High King, with all the company of heaven.
The nourishment of pure love be in my house,
and the roots of repentance.
May we have baskets of love to give,
with cups of mercy for everybody.
Sweet Jesus, be here with us,
with all the company of heaven.
May this meal be full of cheerfulness,
for this is a feast of the great High King,
who is our host for all eternity.

Leader	When you have forgiven each other wrongs
	you do to each other, your Father forgives you.
All	We forgive each other;
	we trust that we are forgiven.

Exchange of the Peace with or without words

| Leader | The peace of Jesus is among us. |
| All | We are one in Jesus. |

A blessing on the meal

Host	King of creation, thank you for this day,
	this food and this company.
	As we eat, may tired limbs be strengthened,
	and tired souls be revived.
	May the freshness and fragrance of the farms
	be with us,
	and the freshness and fragrance of your presence
	cheer us.

A loaf of bread is placed in the centre of the table
The host holds it and the following is said:

Host	On behalf of us all I offer this loaf to God.
All	Let us bless the Lord.
Leader	In our gathering
All	let us bless the Lord.
Leader	As grains of wheat scattered on a thousand fields
	were gathered and became one in this loaf,
All	may we who have been scattered in many places
	become one company in Christ.

| Leader | The seed is Christ's, the granary is Christ's; |
| All | in the granary of God may we be gathered. |

Leader	Bread is a lovely thing to eat,
All	God bless the barley and the wheat.
Leader	A lovely thing to breathe is air,
All	God bless the sunshine everywhere.
Leader	The world is a lovely place to know,
All	God bless the folk who come and go.
Leader	Alive is a lovely thing to be,
All	Giver of life, we say: Bless Thee.

Anon

Reader	Be gentle when you touch bread.
	Let it not lie, uncared for, unwanted.
	So often bread is taken for granted.
	There is such beauty in bread –
	beauty of sun and soil,
	beauty of patient toil.
	Wind and rain have caressed it,
	Christ often blessed it.
	Be gentle when you touch it.

Anon

The bread is passed round and each breaks a piece
When all have taken a piece, these are eaten

Then drinks are passed round

Leader	Drink the water of life; renewing our energy;
	sweetening sour hearts;
Males	God creating and strengthening us;
Females	God nurturing and sustaining us;

Males	filling us all with the gifts of the Spirit;
Females	flowing through us and setting our spirits free.

All may drink

Host The food which we are to eat
is earth, water and sun
coming to us through pleasing plants.
The food which we are to eat
is the fruit of the labour of many creatures.
We are thankful for it.
May it give us health, strength, joy
and may it increase our love.

A Unitarian prayer

All We will be mindful of your presence as we eat.

If there is a full meal, this is now enjoyed
There may be sharing of news and thoughts
There may be teaching, story telling, poetry and music

Before departing

Leader May this meal give new energy to our frames,
new love to our souls.
Refreshed, may we give pleasure
to you and to the world,
and sleep this night in peace.

Shalom
A Weekend Household Meal

This household meal combines Jewish and Celtic prayers (and some of the material in the Agape) with storytelling or Scripture. It may take place weekly, monthly, or to celebrate a special anniversary or season. It may include a meal prepared by the host, each person may bring food to share, or it may simply be a symbolic meal of bread and drinks.

It marks the end of the working week. It is an opportunity to gather together the fragments of the week and to be fully present to one another. It can become an effortless household habit to which friends and neighbours may come, or not, as they wish.

In Jewish tradition the shabat meal on Friday evening marks Sabbath Eve. Examples of shabat meals are included in Michelle Guiness' *A Touch of Seasoning*.

The word shalom, which is sometimes translated as peace, implies personal and communal well-being that is the fruit of living in harmony with self, neighbours, the created world and God.

To celebrate some special event a safari-meal evening may be held. Participants have drinks in one house, and each course in a different house.

Other words may be substituted over the weeks

Host	Come, Lord Jesus, be our guest.
	Stay with us for day is ending.
All	With friend, with stranger, with young, with old,
	be among us tonight.

Host	You invite us, Lord, to share our journeys with you; and even to share your journey, too.
Leader	Let us gather together the fragments of our life journeys and share these in the fellowship of a meal.
All	We come to keep faith with our God, with those who have gone before us, and with one another.
Host	Tonight we thank you for family and friendship, loyalty and love.

Candles are lit by the host who says:

Host   Light of the world, as we light these candles may your truth and love shine in our hearts and dwell in our homes. For in your light we shall see light. May we receive the joy that comes from giving and the peace that comes from receiving.

Leader   When you have forgiven each other the wrongs you do each other, your Father forgives you.

All   We forgive each other; we trust that we are forgiven.

Each greets the other with the word 'shalom' or the word 'peace'

Leader   The peace of the Saviour and the saints is with us.

All   Thanks be to God.

There may be singing, including a song on the theme of shalom

Host   We are your guests.
It is you who keep the generous table.
In trust and friendship and freeing laughter,
in food and drink you draw near.
With blessing bend over this gift
your care does send.
Whoever of this feast does drink,
give them vision brimful running over.

Reader   Bread is a lovely thing to eat,
God bless the barley and the wheat.
A lovely thing to breathe is air,
God bless the sunshine everywhere.
The world is a lovely place to know,
God bless the folk who come and go.
Alive is a lovely thing to be,
Giver of life, we say: Bless Thee.

Anon

A loaf is held up

Reader   Be gentle when you touch bread.
Let it not lie, uncared for, unwanted.
So often bread is taken for granted.
There is such beauty in bread –
beauty of sun and soil,
beauty of patient toil.
Wind and rain have caressed it,
Christ often blessed it.
Be gentle when you touch it.

Anon

*The bread is passed round and each breaks a piece.
When all have taken a piece, these are eaten. Then
drinks are passed round*

Leader	Drink the water of life: renewing our energy;
	sweetening sour hearts;
Men	God creating and strengthening us;
Women	God nurturing and sustaining us;
Men	filling us all with the gifts of the Spirit;
Women	flowing through us and setting our spirits free.

All drink. If there is a full meal, this may follow

Stories are shared. These may be personal experiences of the past week, or they may focus on a theme such as: a lesson learned; a step taken; a fruitful encounter; a discovery made; an evil overcome. Or the story may be told of a person, living or dead, who has inspired personal journeys or whose season it is; those present describe how this speaks to them.

Before departing, hold hands in silence

This may be followed by free prayer, the reading of a Scripture to be used on Sunday or singing

Leader	Sleep in peace.
	Sleep soundly.
	Sleep in love.
	Weaver of dreams
	weave well in you as you sleep.
All	Amen.

Blessings on Meals

Bless, O God, this food.
And if there be any one
who is hungry or thirsty walking outside,
send them in to us
that we may share it with them
as you share yourself with us.

In a world where so many are hungry,
we thank you for this food.
In a world where so many are lonely,
we thank you for this friendship.

May the freshness and fragrance of the farms
be with us as we enjoy this meal.
May the freshness and fragrance of your presence
linger with us as we journey on.

May this food give new energy to tired limbs,
new thoughts to weary minds,
and new warmth to cold hearts.

May the blessing of the five loaves and two fishes,
which you shared out among five thousand,
be with us as we eat,
that we may share our renewed lives
with a needy world.

You who put beam in golden sun,
you who put ear in wheat,
you who put fish in stream and sea
put a grateful heart in me.

Baptism

Introduction

Baptism means immersion. As a fish is immersed in the water, so the Christian is immersed in God. This means we are immersed in the Three Loves that are God's essence. One of these Loves ('the second Person of the Trinity') became manifest as a human being, who is known as Jesus the Christ.

The Bible and the Church also teach that at baptism we are incorporated into Christ (Romans 6:3; Galatians 3:27). Christ is both fully human and fully divine. To be baptised into the human Christ means that we are seeking to become fully human. To be baptised into the divine Christ means that we seek to be christified, to be immersed in God, to share God's life.

Baptism also affirms our true being. At Jesus' baptism he was given a sense of well-being when his divine Father spoke the words 'in you I am well pleased' (Mark 1:11). He was affirmed in the essence of his being because he was rooted in love.

Many people have not known this rooting in love. So we have to be re-rooted. Baptism is therefore a re-rooting in love and an affirmation that we are a child in whom God delights.

In early Christian Ireland there were baptisms with three acts of immersion. An Old-Irish glossator visualised these as three waves. Sometimes there was a single immersion at baptisms in Britain.

In common with the Church elsewhere, a course of instruction was given before baptism. Some Irish texts reveal that St Patrick also looked for grief of heart and evidence of true repentance before he baptised a person. In Patrick's letter to Coroticus there is a reference to the candidates wearing a white veil.

In the Stowe rite the breast and shoulders of the candidates were anointed with oil (chrismated) before baptism, their feet were washed afterwards and they then received Holy Communion. Generally anointing seems to have followed baptism.

There are references to baptisms taking place in wells and rivers as well as in church fonts. Many churches were built next to a good water supply, which met the need of water for baptisms, for regular chanting of praise while standing in water, and (because churches were communities) for the drinking supply of its members. Pioneers like St Patrick deliberately established churches next to wells or rivers.

We have no records of the details of the baptism ceremony in the early Celtic Church. From the Stowe rite, which reflects the gradual Romanisation, it is possible to reconstruct what was probably the sequence of a ninth-century Irish baptism:

- An opening prayer
- A prayer that God would exorcise the devil from each organ of the body and reign within the candidate
- Consecration of salt, exorcism of the water and a prayer
- Renunciation of evil and declaration of the Creed by the candidate
- The administrator breathed on the candidate as a sign of infilling of the Holy Spirit
- Anointing of breast and shoulders with oil in the name of the Trinity

- Asking a second time whether (s)he intended to renounce the devil and his works
- A prayer
- Salt (symbol of cleansing and preserving) is placed in the mouth followed by a prayer
- Second anointing, psalms and prayers
- Font signed with the cross and water is sprinkled
- A deacon interviews them on their belief in God
- Candidates stand in the water and are immersed
- While standing in the water, oil is poured on their heads in the name of the Trinity
- A deacon places a white veil on each head while the priest prays for their forgiveness and blessing
- The candidate is clothed in a white robe while (s)he is asked if (s)he will accept the robe of Christ's righteousness
- Oil put on candidate's hand; prayer that his/her activities might be dedicated to eternal life
- Washing of the candidate's feet while verses from the Psalms and from John 13 are read
- Holy Communion, prayers, thanksgivings and pledges of dedication

In the following service there is only one act of renouncing sin and one anointing follows the baptism.

Foot-washing at baptism died out in most of the western Church, but continued for some time longer in Celtic lands. Since, as Augustine taught, Jesus commanded this as a form of humble service, it seems good to retain a link between the inward grace of baptism and the out-going service this should inspire. We therefore include a symbolic act of service in this service.

We know that Cuthbert, a bishop in the seventh-century Northumbrian Church, laid his hands on those who had recently been baptised (Bede's *Life of Cuthbert*, Chapter 29).

Later, as the practice of infant baptism became established in the western Church, this act of a bishop laying on hands to confirm people in the Holy Spirit was turned into a rite of confirmation.

*Candidates should arrive appropriately dressed
for immersion*

Baptism of a Believer

Preparation

Leader May we be
immersed in the greatness of the Father,
buried in the depths of Christ,
borne along in the flowing of the Spirit.

*There may be opening worship, singing and a prayer,
such as the following, that God would exorcise the
devil from each organ of the body and reign within
the candidate:*

Reader Christ our almighty Deliverer,
expel every evil power from your head,
from your mouth,
from your ears, from your heart, from your body.
May you be set free from all
that would hold or harm,
in every part of your being,
from the crown of your head
to the soles of your feet.
And may he reign in you for ever.

There may be singing

The minister holds a container of salt

Minister Lord, take this salt and make it a sign and seal
of your cleansing and preserving of the believer.

The minister holds a hand over the water

Minister May this water remind us of the water
of the Red Sea in which your people of old

were immersed when they passed over from slavery to freedom. May this water be to us a true sign and seal of your cleansing, renewing and freeing power in our lives.

Teaching, Bible readings or storytelling

The following story may be told:

Storyteller

Soon after Patrick began his mission to the Irish he won the support of Loiguire, King of Connaught, High King of Ireland. The king's virgin daughters came to bathe at a well early one morning and saw, to their amazement, Patrick and a team of priests clothed in white vestments. 'Are you real or from the other world?' they asked. Patrick encouraged them to enquire about the real God rather than about themselves. His reply to their question, 'Who is God?' has become famous as Patrick's Creed. 'Since you are daughters of an earthly king,' Patrick concluded, 'I wish to wed you to the king of heaven.' They asked for instruction, cast off their sins, and were baptised. 'When shall we see Christ's face?' they then asked. 'Unless you taste death and receive the sacrament you shall not see the face of Christ,' Patrick told them. They received the sacrament, and died to their old way of life – some say they physically died. So powerful was the effect that their two druid guides were converted, one at first, the other later.

Declaration of faith

Those to be baptised renounce evil and declare their Christian faith in their own words, through question and answer or in the words prescribed by their Church. The following catechism, based on Patrick's baptism of the daughters of the High King of Ireland, may be used. C = candidates; P = Patrick or priest or pastor.

C   Who is the true God?
P   He is the God of all people.
C   Where is God?
P   God lives in heaven, earth and sea and in all that is
     in them. He inspires, gives life to, directs and
     sustains all. He lights the light of the sun and
     provides the light of the sky. He provides our water
     supplies and the stars above.
C   Is he good-looking? Has he children and money?
P   He has a Son coeternal with himself and like himself.
C   Is he immortal?
P   The Son is not younger than the Father,
     nor the Father older than the Son. The Father,
     the Son and the Spirit are not divided.
C   How may we know him? In what way will he appear?
P   I wish to unite you with the heavenly King, as the
     children of an earthly king are united to him.
C   Is he found in youth or old age?
P   Believe!
C   Tell us how we may believe that we may see him face
     to face.
P   Believe!

C   How may we be prepared to meet him?

P   Do you believe that by baptism you can cast away the sin you have inherited?

C   We believe!

P   Do you believe in life after death?

C   We believe!

P   Do you believe in the resurrection in the day of judgement?

C   We believe!

P   Will you be baptised?

C   We will do as you say.

An assistant breathes on each candidate

Reader   As Jesus breathed on his apostles and said, 'Be filled with the Holy Spirit', so may you be filled with God's Spirit today.

An assistant places salt in each candidate's mouth

Reader   May the tongue that is like a destroying forest fire disappear from your life. Now, in Christ, may your conversation be seasoned with salt, and may you always know when to keep silent, when and what to speak, that your tongue may build up others and bring glory to your God.

There may be singing

Intercession

These may include any of the following:

Leader   For your love for us, nurturing and warm,
which brought us to birth
and has brought us to rebirth,

All   we honour you and give you our love.

Leader   For your love for us, wild and freeing,
which has awakened us to your pulse in nature
and in human life,

All   we honour you and give you our love.

Leader   For your love for us, suffering and patient,
which has brought us through pain,
wept for us in our sins,
and waited for us in our confusion,

All   we honour you and give you our love.

Leader   For your love for us, strong and challenging,
which has called us to risk all for you,
drawn out the best in us and shown us
how to live,

All   we honour you and give you our love.

Leader   Teach us to live in you as fish live in water.
Teach us to be borne of the Spirit as the birds
are borne of the wind.

A candidate

Praying and praising, immersed in your sea of love,
arms stretched like the Saviour's,
cross-like in mercy,
immersed in compassion,

Servant Christ, help us to follow you deep into
the waters of baptism.

A candidate

Help us to follow you into the desert
where we are stripped of the surfeits that distract.
Help us to follow you into your work
of healing the world.

Candidates

We give ourselves to you, God,
today and every day.
All that we are we give you,
all that we do and say.

We give ourselves to you, God,
today with all our being;
in sickness and in health, God,
our feeling and our seeing.

A minister makes the sign of the cross over the water,
dips a sprig, for example, of Rosemary, into it
and sprinkles the people

Minister Jesus says, 'You must be born of water and the
Spirit.' And, 'Streams of life-giving water will
pour out from the heart of the one who believes
in me.'

Minister Into the life of the Father I immerse you,
that he may protect you from harm,
bring you peace and calm.
Into the boundless life of your Maker
I immerse you.

Assistant Into the life of the Son I immerse you,
that he may save you from hell,
keep you washed and well.
Into the sinless life of your Saviour I immerse you.

Minister Into the life of the Spirit I immerse you,
that (s)he may light up your night,
give you power to do right.
Into the endless life of your Guide I immerse you.

Assistant Into the life of the Three I immerse you,
that they may fill you with love,
lift you to heaven above.
Into the selfless love of the Trinity I immerse you.

Each person, suitably clothed for immersion, stands in the water and one person each side immerses them three times in the name of God, Father, Son and Holy Spirit. Children kneel around the place of baptism. Videos and photographs are taken.

Baptiser I/we baptise you in the name of God, the Father, the Son and the Holy Spirit.

All present reach out their hands to pray for the one being baptised. A minister or assistant pours a little oil on the head of each, saying:

Anointer We anoint you in the name of the Three Loves who are the essence of God: Father, Saviour and Holy Spirit. May you be affirmed in your innermost being. Know that you are a much loved child of God and that you have a vocation to serve God and others in the power and wisdom of the Spirit for the rest of your life.

Each baptised person may have a sponsor who places a white robe over them and says:

Sponsor Having laid aside your old life, put on Christ's robe of righteousness so that you will be ready to appear at any time before the One to whom we have to give account.

An assistant marks the palm of the hand of each of the newly baptised with oil and says:

Anointer May all that you do be of eternal worth. As Christ washed the feet of his disciples, may you wash the feet of the world, and serve others in Christ's name.

The newly baptised may make an act of service to someone – for example, clean their shoes or give them a drink or wash the hands or face of a child As they do this verses from the Psalms, and John, chapter 13, may be read

They and the baptisers leave to dry and change clothes, escorted by a sponsor with a towel, etc.

The congregation sings and worships as the newly baptised return

There may now be Holy Communion

At the close

Leader Let us go forward
in the firmness of the Father,
in the forgiveness of the Son,
in the flowing of the Spirit,
in the love of the Three in One.

There may be celebrations

Baptism of an Infant

*When family and friends have gathered, someone may
sing a song, and a priest or another minister may
explain the meaning of baptism*

The signing of the cross

*A minister or parent marks the baby's forehead
with the sign of the cross and says:*

N (name of infant), I mark you with the sign of
the cross.

*Any family member or godparent may make the
sign of the cross on the baby's forehead*

Leader *N (name of infant)*
All may the cross of Christ be always between you
and all that harms you.

God's Word

*A member of the family may read one of the
following passages:*

Reader Matthew 28:18-20; Acts 16:22-34; Ephesians 4:1-6

God's calling to parents

*Other parents may offer encouragement by way
of stories or tell how they make the baptism vows real
for their children. A mother and a father may say
how they pray, play with and listen to their child*

The baptism

A minister, followed by family and friends, takes the baby to a place of water, a baptistery or a font, and dips or pours water on each child saying:

Minister *N*, I baptise you in the name of
the Creator who made you,
the Saviour who gave his life for you,
and the Holy Spirit who is here, now,
and come to live in you.

Three friends, family members or godparents in turn place a drop of water on the infant's forehead with these words:

First A little drop of your Creator, precious one.
Second A little drop of your Saviour, precious one.
Third A little drop of your Guardian Spirit, precious one.
All To bless you with virtue and courage,
in fullness of life everlasting.

The Commitments from the Blessing and Dedication of Infants may be made and the Blessing of a Baby's Future may be said (see below)

There may be singing

Intercession

Leader Lord, your little ones come seeking you in your house – peering round pillars of ancient strength, listening to the sound of bell and organ, scampering up and down the aisles, finding their own routes round and round, guided by your Spirit; fascinated by the latch mechanisms of ancient doors, experimenting with the echo of young voices, in silent awe of beautiful colours telling even more beautiful stories.

Jesus, who called little ones to be with you and they heard your voice beyond the protestations of adults, call again the little ones of this nation to the cradling of your love. May they come wriggling, toddling, straining at the leash, leaning forward from their wheeled transport, giving ear to your call. In this place, Lord, let them hear of your mighty incarnation, your baptism in the Jordan River, your death on a cross for their salvation, your bursting from the spiced tomb – come, you little ones, come!

A lighted candle may be given to the mother or father on behalf of the baby
The following words may be sung to the baby or said by all:

All   Christ as a light illumine and guide you.
Christ as a shield overshadow you.
Christ under you, Christ over you,
Christ beside you on your left and your right,
this day be within and without you,
lonely and meek yet all-powerful.
Be in the mouth of each to whom you shall speak,
in the mouth of each who shall speak to you.
Christ as a light illumine and guide you.

St Patrick's Breastplate,
adapted by John Michael Talbot

Blessing and Dedication of Infants

The earliest accounts of baptism in Celtic lands refer only to believers. Yet by the time the Penitential attributed to Cummian was written in the mid-seventh century, the practice of a formal blessing of an infant by a priest, as a substitute for baptism, incurred a discipline. This suggests (1) that the blessing of infants had been one of the earliest Celtic practices; (2) that when a whole people embraced Christianity their infants were expected to be baptised; (3) that blessings of infants are most appropriate in the context of the home or of unchurched families. The following service is offered in this understanding.

In recent centuries Churches which reject infant baptism provide for the infants of believers to be dedicated, and for their parents to make commitments. This service therefore includes such a commitment. The parents and leader (who may be a minister) should decide beforehand which of the numbered commitments they wish to omit.

Welcome

Leader   We welcome (*names of mother and/or father*) and join them in giving thanks for the gift of (*name of infant*) to be their daughter/son, and to be a new brother/sister for (*names of any siblings or half-brothers and half-sisters of the baby*).

We meet on this special day to celebrate the birth and naming of this child, to witness solemn undertakings on her/his behalf by her/his parents, and to ask God's blessing on this precious life.

Thanks

Leader and parents God our Creator, in giving us this child you have shown us your love. We thank you from our hearts for the joy of this child, for the wonder of its life, for a safe delivery, and for the privilege of being parents.

Naming

Leader *(to the parents)*
You have brought your child to be welcomed into your circle of family and friends. What names have you chosen?

The parents state the names; the leader or a parent may explain the meaning of the names

Commitments

The leader may ask the parent(s) the following questions:

1. **Leader** Will you care for this child, feed and befriend her/him, listen to and play with her/him, keep her/him safe, and daily share your heart with her/him?
Parent(s) I will.

2. **Leader** Will you help your child, by your example and your teaching, to be honest, responsible, and to help others?
Parent(s) I will.

3. Leader Will you respect, encourage and guide her/him, and will you put her/his true needs before your pleasure? Will you try to order your lives so that your child will be surrounded by love and goodness?

Parent(s) I will.

4. Leader For the sake of your child, will you remain together and work at being good friends, even in conflict? Will you say sorry when you are wrong and forgive when you are wronged?

Parent(s) I will.

5. Leader Do you dedicate your child to God?
Parent(s) I do.

6. Leader Do you dedicate yourselves to God, and do you promise, by God's help, to provide a Christian home for this child, to pray with your child, to teach your child about Christ, and to encourage your child to know and serve Christ?

Parent(s) I do.

The leader may ask the family friends the following questions:

1. Leader Will you be a continuing friend to this child and be ready to help in times of special need?
Friends I will.

2. Leader Will you pray for this child and give her/him opportunities to ask questions about your own journey through life?
Friends I will.

The leader asks any sisters, brothers, half-sisters or half-brothers (siblings) the following question:

Leader Will you try to be kind and to share things with her/him and will you treat her/his parents and your parents with respect?

Siblings I will.

The leader asks grandparent(s) the following question:

Leader Will you do your best to give thoughtful support and encouragement as long as you live?

Grandparent(s)
I will.

Leader God bless you and help you carry out these promises.

Words to remember

Reader When God's people were first given guidance as to how to bring up their families, they were told: Remember this! The LORD – and the LORD alone – is our God. Love the LORD your God with all your heart, with all your soul, and with all your strength. Never forget these commands that I am giving you today. Teach them to your children. Repeat them when you are at home and when you are away, when you are resting and when you are working.

Deuteronomy 6:4-7, TEV

A card bearing the above words may be given to the parents to hang above the infant's bedroom door

There may be a song, poem, or music

Reader   They brought children for [Jesus] to touch. The disciples rebuked them, but when Jesus saw this he was indignant, and said to them, 'Let the children come to me; do not try to stop them; for the kingdom of God belongs to such as these. I tell you, whoever does not accept the kingdom of God like a child will never enter it.' And he put his arms round them, laid his hands upon them, and blessed them.

Mark 10:13-16, NEB

A copy of the Gospel of Mark may be presented to the parents as follows:

Leader   We welcome *(name of infant)* as Jesus welcomed children. This book contains the good news of God's love. Read it, for it tells how you and your family may turn from evil, trust in Jesus Christ, and share in God's eternal purpose.

Gifts may be given, and prayers may be said such as the following:

The circling prayer and blessing

A candle may be lit and given to the mother
Everyone stands in a circle around the baby and the parents

Leader   Circle her/him, Lord, keep good within, keep harm without.
Circle her/him, Lord, keep love within, keep hate without.

Any individuals may name something they wish to be kept without

Any   Keep . . . without.

Any individuals may name something they wish to be kept within

Any   Keep . . . within.

The 'Blessing the Baby's Future' (on following pages) may be said when appropriate. If desired, different people may say the following prayers:

First   Father of love, accept the thanksgiving of these parents. May their spirits lifted to you now in humble gratitude, always turn to you for help and strength. Give them wisdom, tenderness, and patience, to guide their child to know right from wrong.

Second   Great God who mothers us all, may (*names of mother and father*) be to each other a strength in need, a comfort in sorrow, a companion in joy. Knit their wills together in your will that they may live together in love, hope and peace all their days.

Third   May you respect one another;
may the goodness of friendship grow in you;
may the love that covers many sins fill you.

If appropriate the baby may be taken into the open air and the leader says the following:

Leader Let all creation join in welcoming this new life. Let us look at the sights and listen to the sounds of creation . . .

Leader God's peace be with you whatever you do;
God's light guide you wherever you go;
God's goodness fill you and help you to grow.

Celebrations may follow

Blessing the Baby's Future

A person may give a flower, plant or anything beautiful and natural and say to the parents:

First   Today we ask that you will try to make your home beautiful so that your child may grow up to appreciate God's beauty.

and to the child:

So today we give you, (*name of child*), this beautiful flower and pray that the personality God has given you will flower into its full beauty.

A person may give a crafted object and say to the parent:

Second   Today we ask that you will try to make your home reflect something of the Creator, by expressing the creativity God has given you and others.

and to the child:

So today we give you, (*name of child*), this crafted present and pray that the creativity God has given you may be fully used.

A person may give to the parents a Bible or book of prayers and say:

Third   Today we ask that you will try in your home to learn about Jesus and to listen to God's voice in the Bible and in your hearts.

and to the child:

So we give you, (*name of child*), this Bible/book
and pray that you will find and follow your calling.

*A person may give to a parent, on behalf of the
baby, a white candle, saying:*

Fourth   Today we ask that you will make your home a
place of faith which radiates the light of Christ.

and to the child:

So we give you, (*name of child*), this candle and
pray that you may shine as a light in the world.

All   Christ as a light illumine and guide you.
Christ as a shield overshadow you.
Christ under you,
Christ over you,
Christ beside you on your left and your right,
this day be within and without you,
lonely and meek yet all-powerful.
Be in the mouth of each to whom you shall speak,
in the mouth of each who shall speak to you.
Christ as a light illumine and guide you.

St Patrick's Breastplate,
adapted by John Michael Talbot

Renewal of Baptism

Find out the date of your baptism. On the anniversary you
could go to a well, river, or a baptismal chapel in a church
and invite a friend to say this prayer for you
Then you could say it for your friend's baptismal anniversary

Ever-creating God,
in the beginning you gave water to the earth
as a source of life and blessing.
Its energies and cleansing properties
give birth to the world of nature
and sustain human life.

Bless this water to remind us
of our baptism in Christ.

Strengthen us on our journey through life
and remind us of the vision
your Son asked us to proclaim.

The promises made at baptism to turn from sin
and believe in the Christian faith are repeated

Water may be sprinkled on the person(s) or they
may stand in water or be immersed. If so the
leader says:

Leader   We renew your baptism into God, affirming
Father, freeing Saviour, flowing Spirit.

Repeat some of the prayers from the baptism service

Weddings

A menu of suggestions that may be woven around the
statutory declarations required by a state or church

A prayer for the bride and groom to repeat
in the weeks before the wedding

Marriage Maker, make me a match!
Fire of Triune Love,
let me move from one to three:
I –you – and s/he.

W. J. Fitzgerald.

The setting before the service

A wild goose or dove (symbols of God's Spirit) may be depicted on a white drape that faces the people, with a coracle or sail each side of it (symbols of the separate lives of the bridge and groom until now). As the groom takes his seat chanters invoke the Holy Spirit (for example, Veni, Sancte Spiritus – Come, Holy Spirit), and they continue to do this as the bride is escorted up the aisle.

Before the start of a wedding service

Open our eyes to your presence.
Open our ears to your call.
Open our hearts to your love.

A welcome followed by singing or music

(chosen by the bridal couple)

After the entrance of the bride as she stands beside the groom

Most powerful Spirit of God,
come down upon us and subdue us.
From heaven,
where the ordinary is made glorious
and glory seems but ordinary,
bathe us
with the brilliance
of your light
like dew.

Before a Bible reading

The minister may lead the bridal couple in a walk around the person who will read the Gospel from the Bible, which the reader holds up. This is a symbol of the journey through life which they are about to begin together. It is a way of saying, 'We do not know where our journey will lead, but wherever it leads, God's Word will be central to it.'

A story

There may be a story such as that of Isaac and Rebekah, recorded in Genesis 24

Homily

*There may be a homily or words such as the following
may be read*

A good marriage must be created.
In a marriage, the little things are the big things . . .
It is never being too old to hold hands.
It is remembering to say, 'I love you' at least once a day.
It is never going to sleep angry.
It is having a mutual sense of values and common goals.
It is standing together and facing the world.
It is forming a circle of love that gathers others in.
It is speaking words of appreciation and demonstrating
  gratitude in thoughtful ways.
It is having the capacity to forgive and forget.
It is giving each other space in which each can grow.
It is a common search for the good and the beautiful.
It is not only marrying the right person – it is being the
  right partner.

Anon

Before the vows

There may be a time of reflection focusing on the bride
and groom, to the accompaniment of background music.
During this anyone may write down prayers, sayings or
good wishes, or draw a picture on pieces of paper that are
provided.

*Here is an example of a prayer that can be written out
on a card and given or read out:*

May the Father take you in his fragrant clasp of love,
in every up and every down of your life.

The love and affection of God be with you,
the love and affection of the angels be with you,
the love and affection of the saints in heaven be with you.
The love and affection of your friends on earth be with you,
to guard you, to cherish you,
to bring you to your eternal fulfilment.

Exchange of candles

Before the service one larger and two smaller candles may be placed on a stand near the place where the bride and groom will make their vows. A main candle, representing Christ, the Light of the World, is already lit before the service. A taper is brought from the main lighted candle, and given to the groom.

> *The groom takes and lights one small candle
> and says to the bride:*

Groom This candle that I light is a sign of all that I am. I came into being enfolded in the light of God's love. It burns brightly with the flame of my hopes and dreams. It is a sign of the undying flame of love I have for you.

> *The groom gives the lighted candle to the bride
> who places it in the place of her unlit candle,
> which she then holds as she says the same*

Bride This candle that I light is a sign of all that I am. I came into being enfolded in the light of God's love. It burns brightly with the flame of my hopes and dreams. It is a sign of the undying flame of love I have for you.

The marriage vows

The couple hold hands and each says to the other the words required by statute in the country where the wedding takes place. They may write their own words to follow or incorporate the statutory wording.

Two examples follow

A   And as the stars in the sky and the tides in the sea
     are constant and true, I pledge myself to you
     in faithfulness and love.

B   And as the stars in the sky and the tides in the sea
     are constant and true, I pledge myself to you
     in faithfulness and love.

or

A   When I walk, will you walk alongside me?
     When I kneel, will you kneel with me?
     When I fall, will you help me to my feet?
     And if I forget, will you help me remember?
     And as each night I lie down to sleep,
     will you lie down to sleep beside me?

B   I will.

     If I fail to see, will you bring me understanding?
     And if I cease to speak, will you talk for me?
     When I need to rest, will you find me peace?
     When I am lost without, will you find me within?
     And when the sun shines down on each new day,
     will you help me to find the far horizon?

A   I will.

Exchange of rings

First My ring is a sign of love never ending.
Second Mine is a circle of true belonging.

Each places a ring on the other's finger

First A circle of gold in joy and sorrow.
Second A circle of gold today and tomorrow.

Joining hands after the vows

May you be bound with unbreakable bonds of love
to one another.
May you be bound with unbreakable bonds of love
to your God.
May your love for each other
reflect the three limitless loves in God.

*If a minister wraps around the couple's hands a stole or piece
of cloth that symbolises the Divine, the minister may pray:*

May you be bound together in God and wrapped
in Divine love.

A bridal blessing after the vows

May the Father take you in God's fragrant clasp of love.
May the Virgin's Son guide you through the maze of life.
May the generous Spirit release forgiving love within you.
Hour by hour, by day and by night, in joy and in failure,
may each man and each woman who are saints in heaven
urge you on to complete your course.

or

This cross be over your mouths,
that you may speak to each other what is in your hearts.
This cross be over your hands,
that your touch may ever be tender.

or

May your love be as constant as the stars above,
as solid as the rock below.

People may clap as the bride and groom kiss each other

Holy Communion

The couple may move forward, kneel and receive the bread and wine of Holy Communion. If desired others may also receive

Blessing the people

Minister Your friends and family have blessed you by
their presence. Now you, who have been joined
in order to be a blessing to the world, will take
God's blessing to them.

During singing or music the couple may then each take a basket of blessed bread and give a piece to each person present. Or they may circle the congregation holding the lighted marriage candle between them. Or they may hand out sweets or a flower to each person

There may be singing and words of encouragement

Prayers

Couple Lord,
let our memory
provide no shelter
for grievance against each other.

Lord,
let our heart provide no harbour
for hatred of each other.

Lord,
let our tongue
be no accomplice
in the judgement of each other.

Reader Beauty of friendship grow between you,
friendship without guile,
friendship without malice,
friendship without striving.

Reader *holding a cross*
This cross be over your eyes,
that you may see each other's needs.

God's own presence with you stay,
Jesus to shield you in the fray,
Spirit to protect you from all ill,
Trinity there guiding you still.

On sea or land, in ebb or flow,
God be with you wherever you go.
In flow or ebb, on land or sea,
God's great might your protection be.

*A prayer for the new household that they are to create
in the community:*

Reader May you be host to the great High King,
with all the company of heaven.
The sustenance of pure love be in your house,
the roots of repentance in your house.
Baskets of love be yours to give,
with cups of mercy for all the company here.
May sweet Jesus, and all the company of heaven,
be there with you.

Signing and singing

*While the bridal party sign the registers
there is singing or music that sustains the sense of
God's Presence such as the following:*

When his children come together
and are joined in holy truth
the angels are rejoicing night and day.

Blessings

Leader May the road rise to meet you.
May the wind be always at your back.
May the sun shine warm upon your face.
The rain fall soft upon your fields of endeavour
and until we meet again
may God hold you
in the hollow of his hand.

May the Three of limitless love pour upon you
tenderly and graciously every day of your life.

The reception

Celtic Christians have a strong sense of place. It is worth giving thought to a place that combines eating, celebration, prayerfulness and scenery worth capturing in the photographs

A grace before the wedding feast

King of creation, we bless you for
the love that comes to flower this day,
the earth that brings us this food,
the friendship that has drawn this company.
May we feast in the presence of our eternal host,
bringing cupfuls of kindness and platefuls of love.

Dying, Funerals and Wakes*

As the end of the journey begins

In the Celtic tradition it is important to become a friend of death. When a person is frail, and may be approaching the end of their earthly journey, memories or songs may be shared.

A holding cross may be given to the frail person and another held by the person by their side. Prayers such as the following from the Hebrides may be said by the person apparently nearing journey's end or by a friend:

As you were there at my life's beginning,
be there again at my journey's end.

As you were there at my soul's shaping,
be there again at its final bend.

May the seven angels of the Holy Spirit
and the two guardian angels
shield me this and every night
till light and dawn shall come.

Full tide, ebb tide, how life's beat must go. *(David Adam)*
Teach me to go with your tides
and allow you, the Creator of tides and time,
to carry me in your love.

---

* There is more extensive material on dying, funerals and wakes in *Before We Say Goodbye: Preparing a Good Death* by Ray Simpson (HarperCollins 2001)

Saviour and Friend, how wonderful you are,
my companion upon the changeful way,
the comforter of its weariness,
my guide to the Eternal Town,
the welcome at its gate.

When my time comes, may I recognise you, who are greater than myself, under the species of each alien or hostile force that seems bent on destroying or uprooting me.

When I suddenly awaken to the fact that I am ill or growing old, when the ill that is to diminish me or carry me off strikes from without or is born within me, above all, at that last moment when I am losing hold of myself and am absolutely passive within the hands of the great unknown forces that have formed me, in all those dark moments, O God, may I understand that it is you who are painfully parting the fibres of my being in order to penetrate to the very marrow of my substance and bear me away within yourself.

You are a loving, active principle of purification and detachment. The more the future opens before me like some dizzy abyss or dark tunnel, the more confident I may be of yielding myself and being assimilated by your body, Jesus.

You who are the irresistible and vivifying force; grant to me something more precious even than the grace for which all faithful pray: teach me to treat my death as the final act of communion.

Teilhard de Chardin, adapted

Beside the dying person

In a Celtic tradition inspired by the Scottish Highlands and Islands, blessings are said over a dying person by a relative or soul friend, along with others. These death blessings are sometimes known as 'soul leading' or 'soul peace'. The soul peace should be said slowly, all present joining the dying person in asking the Three Persons of the Trinity and the saints in heaven to receive the departing soul.

During the prayer the soul friend makes the sign of the cross on the dying person's forehead or lips. Even with people with little religious background a well-known Bible passage, hymn or one of these prayers may be said, and a cross may be held in front of them.

Death with oil, death without pain.
Death with joy, death without fear.
Death with light, death without death.
Death with gladness, death without horror.
Death with penitence, death without grieving.

Carmina Gadelica

Alone with none but you, my God, I journey on my way.
What need I fear, when you are near,
O King of night and day?
More safe am I within your hand
than if a host did round me stand.

Attributed to Columba

Father who sought you, Christ who bought you,
Spirit who taught you, hold you in Trinity's heart of love.

May shining souls and all the risen ones beckon you on:
(include appropriate examples or the following)
Gentle Aidan and holy Hilda, generous Brigid and kindly
Cuthbert, holy and wise ones to accompany you.

On hearing of a person's death

Personal acts of remembrance

*A candle is lit in memory of the deceased person. A memento,
flower or card is placed by the candle. Some time is spent in
silence remembering them*

*A Pannikhida (the Orthodox term for a service of prayer for
those who have passed on) such as the following may be said.
The prayers for use at funerals may be used instead*

God of tender consolations, take this your dearest soul,
that in the company of heaven
s/he may pass from the fading light of earth
into the fullness of everlasting life.

Take your servant from our fretful ways
into your unending peace.

Grand her/him your peace past knot of death,
grant her/him your love unfolding past knot of death.
Sun of suns, pour healing grace upon her/him,
shed light eternal on her/him.

Bathed in your light, immersed in your presence,
may s/he know peace of deepest sea,
peace of Trinity.

Lord have mercy.
Christ have mercy.
Lord have mercy.
N (speak name of deceased)

The perishable is clothed with the imperishable.
You are changed.

The mortal is clothed with the immortal.
You are changed.

May you go forward and journey into the heart of God.
Father who sought you, Christ who bought you,
Spirit who taught you,
hold you in Trinity's heart of love.

Joy and praise to your Creator.
Alleluia, alleluia, to the ages of ages. Amen.

Prayers for use at funerals

Introductory words

God be blessed for the wonder of a life.

Jesus said: My peace I leave with you.
Let not your hearts be troubled or afraid.

The lights fade, the rumble of creation diminishes,
mists descend and blanket out what has been.
Our Creator calls us to release the one whom we love
from this world.
Our Saviour calls us to remain united with him who alone
can help the one who has left us.

Since it was you, O Christ, who bought each soul –
at the time it gave up its life, at the time of returning to clay;
at the time of the shedding of blood,
at the time of severing the breath,
at the time you delivered judgement –
may your peace be on your ingathering of souls,
Jesus Christ, Son of gentle Mary,
your peace be upon your own ingathering.

There may be readings, poems, singing or sharing of memories.
Bible readings may include 1 Corinthians 15:42-49

The soul's onward journey

Go forward on your journey, O loved child of God.
May you pass from the darkness of mortal death
into the fullness of life eternal.
May you pass from our fretful ways
into the creative peace of divine partnership.
May you pass from the knots of life and death
into the seamless tapestry of God's healing grace.

Go forth upon your journey from this world,
in the name of God the Father who created you;
in the name of Jesus Christ who died for you;
in the name of the Holy Spirit who illumines you;
in friendship with God's saints, aided by the holy angels.
May you rest this day in the peace and love
of your eternal home.

Traditional, adapted

In the name of the all powerful Father,
in the name of the all loving Son,
in the name of the pervading Spirit
I command all spirit of fear to leave you,

I break the power of unforgiven sin in you,
I set you free from dependence upon human ties,
that you may be as free as the wind,
as soft as sheep's wool, as straight as an arrow;
and that you may journey into the heart of God.

Prayer for the bereaved

O God in whose arms we die, who brought us to birth,
in our grief and shock contain, sustain and comfort us,
embrace us with your love,
give us hope in our confusion and grace to let go.

At wakes

*Wakes are gatherings of the deceased person's friends and
family to remember and celebrate their lives by eating,
drinking, recounting memories, telling stories, singing songs*

Wake-time, sorrow-sharing time.
Wake-time, story-telling time.
Wake-time, vigil-keeping time.
Wake-time, embracing time.

>   *William J. Fitzgerald*

We will have good weather after the final raindrop.

>   *An Irish saying*

And when the earth shall claim your limbs,
then shall you truly dance.

>   *Kahlil Gibran*

Death is not extinguishing the light.
It is putting out the lamp because the dawn has come.

>   *Rabindranath Tagore*

Other Rites of Passage

Prayer for an aborted baby

Parent   Dear God, full of a tender mother's heart, this
child who was lost was yours and mine, and I
am yours.*

You know about the pressures,
the difficulties, my weakness.
I am sorry for my neglect and lack of love.
I ask your forgiveness.
I thank you for your understanding.
Now I place my child in to your loving care.

Minister/Soul friend

We release (*name of child*)
into your loving arms, O God.
Bring her/him to wholeness
in your eternal kingdom.*

Parent   I wish to name before you my child
who was born on (*date*).
I name her/him . . .
I ask you to heal her/him of any shock or hurt
(s)he has carried as a result of the way (s)he died.*

*A flower, plant, plaque or cross may be placed in a
place of remembrance†*

---

* These sentences may also be used for a miscarried baby
† These symbolic acts may also be used for a miscarried baby

The minister or soul friend holds a crucifix or cross
in front of the parents and says:

Minister/Soul friend

Christ died on a cross and came back
to bring us all life.
May this cross come between you and the past.
May Christ hold you in this life
and hold (*name of child*) in the life beyond.

May you find healing of past wounds.
May you walk free into fruitful paths.

God be with you each day of your life ahead.

Prayer at the time of divorce

Grant us
acceptance of pain without bitterness,
grieving of loss without blame,
forgiveness for frailty without remorse,
renewal of trust without fear.

Blessing on an anniversary

Joy of memory be yours today.
Joy of creation be yours today.
Joy of goodness be yours today.
Joy of friendship be yours today.
Joy of giving be yours today.
Joy of maturing be yours today.
Joy of eternal life be yours today.

House Blessings

Reader   Unless the Lord builds the house,
              its builders toil in vain.

                                        Psalm 127:1

Leader   God our Protector, we ask your blessing on this
              home and all who live in it. May its doors be
              open to those in need and its rooms be filled
              with kindness. May love dwell within its walls,
              and joy shine from its windows. May this house
              be built upon Christ the Rock of rocks so that
              no onslaught can undermine it and no ill-wind
              can unsettle it. May it be a sanctuary and a sign
              of hope.

Reader   Love the Lord your God with all your heart,
              and all your soul and all your strength. Write
              these words on your hearts. Repeat them to
              your children, and talk about them when you sit
              down in your home, and when you walk in the
              street; when you lie down and when you rise up.
              Hold fast to them as a sign. Write them on your
              doorposts.

                                    Deuteronomy 6:4-9

*The Jewish Mezuzah (the text of Deuteronomy 6:4-9
contained on a scroll or in a box) may be fixed above
a door post. Or a cross, icon, or Bible text may be
positioned in a place chosen by the household*

*A Celtic (circular) cross is held and the following
prayer is said:*

Leader   May the cross of Christ set this place free
from the influences of the past and may
all the unseen powers here acclaim him.

All   Circle this place by day and by night
in winter's cold and summer's light.
Keep within Christ's healing balm.
Keep without all that would harm.

*A sprig – for example, of Rosemary – may be
dipped in a bowl of water and sprinkled on the
main or each door. Or doors may be signed with
the cross by a finger that has been dipped in the
water*

*Any of the following prayers may be used room by
room:*

Kitchen

May the Son of Mary possess all who work
amid the clatter of this place. Bring forth
fullness in the cooking, and working.

Dining room

May you eat and drink mindful of the good
fruits of creation. Here may you be conscious of
the presence of the Bountiful Giver, your eternal
host. May the spirit of gratitude and fellowship
mark your meals.

Living room

May the God of Three Loves free all who meet
here to forgive from their hearts, to flower as
persons and to be at home with themselves.

Workroom

> May all that is done here reflect the creativity and
> order of creation. Inspire . . . the research and
> design, the reading and writing, the creating
> and planning.

Playroom

> May those who play in this room have fun, and
> make those they play with happy.

Bedroom

> God be with you in your sleeping and dreaming.
> May there be love in your lying
> and life in your rising.
> May that part of you that did not grow more
> whole by day, grow at night.

Washroom

> The word of Christ be in your mouth
> as you clean your teeth.
> The beauty of Christ be in your face
> as you comb your hair.
> The love of Christ flow through your being
> as you wash your frame.

Pets' place

> May the cat(s) purr with the pleasures
> of friendship.
> May the dog(s) wag their tails with the delights
> of meeting.
> May *(name the pet)* be happy and healthy
> and give much pleasure.

Garden

> Bless the creatures that shall live here,
> the birds that shall chirp here,

the seedlings that shall grow here,
the neighbours you shall greet here,
and all who overlook here.

Any place of disquiet

Almighty and redeeming God,
you are stronger than the elements,
stronger than the shadows,
stronger than the fears,
stronger than human wills,
stronger than the spirits;
we enthrone you in this place
and lift you up with our praise.

There may be praise or prophetic prayer

An Annual House Blessing

*In the Celtic tradition this takes place on St Brigid's Day
(1 February) at the start of the Celtic year but other times may
be chosen. On St Brigid's Day, St Brigid's crosses are made (of
reeds or even of drinking straws) and may be distributed to
homes of neighbours and friends*

The house door

Reader   God make the door of this house wide enough
to receive all who need human fellowship here,
narrow enough to shut out envy, pride and
strife. Make its threshold smooth enough to be
no stumbling block to children or straying feet,
but rugged and strong enough to turn back the
tempter's power. God make the door of this
house the gateway to your eternal kingdom.

Anon

Resident We invite you, O Christ, to be the Leader
of this household and of everything in it.

*This prayer, sometimes attributed to St Bridget,
may be read by a resident:*

I would prepare a feast and be host to the great
High King, with all the company of heaven.

The sustenance of pure love be in my house,
the roots of repentance in my house.
Baskets of love be mine to give,
with cups of mercy for all the company.
Sweet Jesus, be there with us,
with all the company of heaven.
May cheerfulness abound in the feast, the feast
of the great High King, my host for all eternity.

Reader Protecting Father be at your doors.
Welcoming angels be on your floors.

Guiding Saviour be in your screens.
Holy angels be in your dreams.

Gracious Spirit be in your head.
Guarding angels be above your bed.

The Friendly Three be a covering above.
Make your house a place of love.

First May this house
be fragrant with the presence of the Lord,
overflow with the gratitude of his people,
echo with the sounds of joy.

Second   Circle this house, Lord, by day and by night,
             in winter's dark and summer's light.
             Keep joy within, keep blame without.
             Keep love within, keep shame without.

Third   O King of stars!
             Whether my house be dark or bright,
             it will not be closed against anybody;
             may Christ not close his house against me.

                                                 Irish

Departures and Journeys

*This pattern of prayer may be used when a person leaves a
household, job or locality, or sets out on a new journey.
L = any who are leaving and setting out*

Letting go

Reader   Before we embark on this new journey let us release
to God those things that we have left behind.

L   We release into your hands, O God, our homes:
those whom we love and care for,
those who have hurt us and left us;
any who feel vulnerable without us.

Reader   Merciful One who mothers us all,
you love those whom we love.

L   We release into your hands
those we have supported
and those who have depended upon us.

Reader   We release into your hands, O God,
the work we shall leave behind.

L   The pressures that weary us,
the problems that would pursue us,
the things we have neglected,
the tasks left unfinished.

Reader   Before you set out on a new venture,
we pray for past failures to be forgiven,
for wounds to be healed,
for confusions to be resolved,

for ignorance to be dispelled,
for relationships to be treasured.

Forgiveness for past failures may be declared

There may be singing

God's Word

Reader   Philippians 3:7-14

There may be singing

A personal litany

The path I travel, Christ travels.
May the place to which I go
be without regret.
May the Trinity protect me wherever I stay.
In every dealing may shining angels walk with me
and be a clear presence,
and may no one's poison get to me.
May the nine orders of heaven's company
favour me with their presence.
May I arrive safely at each destination.
May the time spent not be wasted.
May every journey be smooth;
may men, women and children welcome me.
A truly good journey.
How well the good Lord guides us on our course.

Eighth or ninth century (paraphrased)

May this journey be easy and profitable.
Holy Christ, protect me from demons
and human onslaughts.
May Jesus and the Father and the Holy Spirit
make us holy.
May the mysterious God
who does not hide away in darkness,
may the bright King save us.
May the cross of Christ and Mary
guard us on the journey.
May we not have mishap;
may the journey be successful and easy.

Sometimes attributed to Columba

Protecting and envisioning

*Those present stand in a circle around the
departing person or the Reader circles them
with their finger*

Reader   We draw a circle of love around you
to protect you from harm,
the Trinity of power to be your strong right arm.
The Father who bore you,
the Saviour who bought you,
the Spirit who taught you,
hold you firm.

Reader   Let us now invite God
to inspire your and our expectations.

Lord, nothing is impossible to you.
You can raise the dead. Raise us up, we pray.

God of surprises, give us a spirit of expectancy
for new horizons to dawn,
for fresh shafts of light to illumine dark corners,
for you to open up the Scriptures to us,
for growth in love, in patience,
in understanding and in humour,
for good experiences in worship,
for a new dawn in your Church,
for an empowering of your people.

L   Risen Christ,
you have called, and the call has been heard.
Help us to be fully present to you
in this moment of choice
and in every moment of the journey ahead.

Silence

Reader   Circle (*name person*) in this moment of
transition.
Keep peace within, keep evil out.
Keep light within, keep dark without.

*All may circle those who are to leave and repeat
this or other circling prayers or pray silently*

Reader   The Sacred Three your force field be,
the Father's heart,
the Saviour's mind,
the Spirit's strength,
now until eternity.

First Voyage of the Coracle

Prayers and trial promises for those being admitted to the Community of Aidan and Hilda

Before taking the first voyage of the coracle an aspirant makes a personal Rule of Life with the help of a soul friend. This applies the ten principles in the Community of Aidan and Hilda's Way of Life to their present circumstances and temperament. The aspirant also examines their life and writes down sins and distractions they wish to leave behind. They have this list and their Personal Rule with them

Leader In the presence of the sending Father,
    in the presence of the saving Son,
    in the presence of the anointing Spirit,
    in the presence of the Three in One.

    Grant, O God, that your Church in this land
    may be true to its birthright. And kindle in us
    the adventure of obedience, the single eye, the
    generous, loving spirit which marked Aidan,
    Hilda and your Celtic saints.

Thanksgiving

In a full service selected verses from the Psalms such as the following may be read

Reader Psalm 136:1-9, 23-26
All   (*after each verse*)
    Whose loves endures for ever.

There may be singing

Philippians 3:7-14

Confession of things we leave behind

Aspirants We confess to you, O Lord, the things we have
wrongly held on to – possessions, affections, habits
and attitudes, which now we leave behind . . .

> *Aspirants may name these in silence or aloud,*
> *and may kneel before a cross and symbolically*
> *leave their list there*

Minister Forgiveness is declared.

A reading from the voyage of Brendan

Reader Brendan chose fourteen monks from his
community, took them to the chapel, and made
this proposal to them: 'My dear fellow soldiers
in the spiritual war, I beg your help because my
heart is set upon a single desire. If it be God's
will, I want to seek out the Island of Promise of
which our forebears spoke. Will you come with
me? What are your feelings?' As soon as he had
finished speaking, the monks replied with one
voice: 'Father, your desire is ours also.' When all
was ready Brendan ordered his monks aboard,
the sail was hoisted, and the coracle was swept
out to sea. For the next two weeks the wind was
fair, so that they did no more than steady the
sail. But then the wind fell, and they had to row,

day after day. When their strength eventually failed, Brendan comforted them: 'Have no fear, brothers, for God is our captain and our pilot; so take in the oars, and set the sail, letting him blow us where he wills.'

The commitments

Leader Brothers and sisters, God is calling you to leave behind everything that stops you setting sail in the ocean of God's love. You have heard the call of the Wild Goose, the untamable Spirit of God: be ready for the Spirit to lead you into wild, windy or well-worn places in the knowledge that God will make them places of wonder and welcome.

God is giving you the vision of a spoiled creation being restored to harmony with its Creator, of a fragmented world becoming whole, of a weakened church being restored to its mission, of lands being healed and lit up by the glorious Trinity.

Remember the words of Christ: Unless a person dies to themselves, takes up their cross, and follows me they cannot be my disciple.

So I ask you:
Do you believe God is calling you to become a member of the Community of Aidan and Hilda?

Aspirant I do.

Leader Do you leave behind all that comes between you and Christ's call?

Aspirant I do.

Leader   Do you forgive all who come between you
and Christ's call?

Aspirant I do.

*Each aspirant places their personal Rule
before a cross or an altar and says:*

Aspirant I give myself without reservation to God, the
Three of limitless love. I seek to know Christ
better and make him better known, to live
simply that others may simply live, to overcome
evil with good, and to follow the example of
Aidan, Hilda and other saints.

I commit myself to simplicity, chastity and the
honouring of those I am responsible to.

I undertake, as God permits, to follow a daily
rhythm of prayer, work, and re-creation, to meet
with my soul friend and to make an annual retreat.

I will pray for and meet with the Community,
using its Prayer Diary and patterns of prayer.

*There is silence during which each new member
prostrates themself or kneels in prayer*

Leader   May the Father's heart be yours;
may the Christ-like qualities
of Aidan and Hilda be yours;
may the signs and wonders of the Spirit be yours.
In stillness or storm, be always vigilant, waiting,
sharing, praising, blessing.
Sail forth across the ocean of God's world,
knowing both the frailty of your craft
and the infinite riches of your God.

The leader, on behalf of the Community, welcomes the new member with these words:

Leader We receive you with joy as a member of the Community and into the fellowship of Aidan, Brendan, Hilda and their fellow saints through the ages. God equip you for service in this Way. May you bind up what is fragmented and heal what is wounded.

The Voyager is presented with a Community cross, a copy of the Way of Life arranged for daily reading, a certificate and a sample of the Community's patterns of prayer

There may be laying on of hands with informal words of prayer, scripture, encouragement, poetry. These may include Isaiah 43:1-3a and the following:

Rhymes from a Lindisfarne monk

Reader He is my king, in my heart he's hid,
he is my joy, all joys amid.
I am a drop in his ocean lost,
his coracle I, on his wide sea tossed,
a leaf in his storm.

The book of his praise in my wallet slung,
the cloak of his friendship round me flung,
hither and thither about I'm blown,
my way an eddy, my rest a stone,
and he my fire.

My meat his work and my drink his will,
he is my song, my strength, my skill,
and all folk my lovers in good and ill
through him my desire.

In the track of the wind I trace his feet,
and none of his coming was e'er so fleet,
so sweet.

Often my heart is a heavy stone,
mocked, trodden under and spat upon,
my way a mirk, and I alone, alone.

Then in my heart flames a climbing star
as his pilgrim feet come flashing far
to bring me where the blessed are.
He is the cleft in the dark sky riven
whereby I may leap to the bending heaven
through the storm.

Marjorie Milne of Glastonbury

*There may be creative activity and singing
ending with these prayers*

Reader Jesus who stopped the wind and stilled the waves,
grant you calm in the storm times;
Jesus, Victor over death and destruction,
bring safety on your voyage;
Jesus of the purest love, perfect companion,
bring guarding ones around you;
Jesus of the miraculous catching of fish,
and the perfect lakeside meal,
guide you finally ashore.

Leader   The mantle of Aidan be upon you,
the mantle of Hilda too,
the mantle of Christ from your crown to your feet.
The God of life be your champion and leader.
You shall not be left in the hand of the wicked;
you shall not be bent in the court of the false;
you shall rise victorious above them,
as rise victorious the crests of the waves.

Voyage of the Coracle
Annual Renewal of First Vows

I renew the commitments made when I took the Voyage of
the Coracle on *(date)*
and the Way of Life of the Community of Aidan and Hilda,
and I offer my personal Rule of Life for this year.

I will seek to wholeheartedly follow Jesus Christ
in the strength of Trinity,
in the spirit of Celtic Saints,
living by Scripture's guidance,
in soul friend's confidence,
in life's rhythms,
in overcoming prayer,
in simplicity of life,
in stewardship of creation,
in the healing of the world,
in stream of God's Spirit,
in solidarity with all,
in sharing with others.

BLESSING THE EARTH

Introduction

God names the first man Adamah (Adam), which means 'earth' (Genesis 2:7). In other words, human beings contain within themselves the whole earth. Jesus Christ, whom St Paul names as 'the second Adam' (1 Corinthians 15:47) comes from heaven, yet contains within his humanity the whole evolving earth story and its future. Jesus is that Word of God (logos) through whom and in whom all things are (John 1:1-3). In the cosmic Jesus is included the whole earth community, now groaning in anticipation of its coming total fulfilment (Romans 8:19-23).

The early Church, secure in its Jewish roots, understood this. Several centuries passed. Whereas Augustine taught that creation was an act of God's power, Celtic Christians saw it as an act of God's love. The Celtic Christians expressed this in the way they lived and prayed and in their poetry. Reflecting on the nature poetry of the Irish ascetics, Kenneth Jackson wrote:

> The woodland birds might sing to him around his cell, but through it all . . . is the understanding that the birds and hermit are joining together in an act of worship; to him the very existence of nature was a song of praise in which he himself took part by entering into harmony with nature.
>
> *Studies in Early Celtic Nature Poetry,*
> Kenneth Jackson (Cambridge, 1935)

A catechism from the eighth century or earlier runs like this:

Question What is best in this world?

Answer To do the will of our Maker.

Question What is his will?

Answer That we should live according to the laws of his creation.

Question	How do we know those laws?
Answer	By study – studying the Scriptures with devotion.
Question	What tool has our Maker provided for this study?
Answer	The intellect which can probe everything.
Question	And what is the fruit of study?
Answer	To perceive the eternal Word of God reflected in every plant and insect, every bird and animal, and every man and woman.

In the early myths of the pre-Christian Celts the god of the tribe mates with the goddess of the earth. Our forebears instinctively understood that the marriage of the human population with the fertile soil is necessary to the well-being of both. In the light of Christian revelation, that instinct can be seen as true, though 'the marriage' needs to be redeemed. Columbanus, who taught 'Understand, if you want to know the Creator, created things', also observed that 'If you trample on creation, creation will trample on you'.

Maximus the Confessor (d. 662) taught that the Creator-Logos has implanted in each created thing a characteristic logos, a 'thought' or 'word', which is the divine presence in that thing, God's intention for it, its inner essence, which makes it to be distinctively itself and at the same time draws it towards God. By virtue of this indwelling logos, each created thing is not just an object but a personal word addressed to us by the Creator. Thus the second Person of the Trinity acts as an all-embracing and unifying cosmic Presence.

St Isaac the Syrian (d. 700) taught that a merciful heart is 'a burning of heart for all creation, whether for people, for birds, for animals, for demons, for every creature. From the memory and contemplation of creatures the eyes stream with tears, and from compassion and pity the heart of the merciful person is moved to grief, and is unable to bear, to see, or to hear of any injury, or of anything grievous occurring in creation. It is for this reason that at all times such a person prays with tears for the dumb beasts, for the enemies of truth, and for those who do him injury. He prays that God may protect them and show mercy. He prays even for the creeping things, out of his great pity, which moves his heart abundantly.' (Discourse 81)

This way of seeing the creation drained away when bureaucratic ways came to dominate the minds as well as the machinery of the medieval Church, but it was never lost. The Rhine mystic Hildegaard of Bingen (1098-1179) records these remarkable words addressed to her by the Holy Spirit:

I, the highest and fiery power,
I have kindled every living spark
and I have breathed out nothing that can die . . .
I . . . am the fiery life of the divine essence –
I flame above the beauty of the fields;
I shine in the waters;
in the sun, the moon and the stars, I burn.
And by means of the airy wind
I stir everything into quickness
with a certain invisible life which sustains all . . .
I, the fiery power, lie hidden in these things
and they blaze from me,
just as a man is continually moved by his breath
and as the fire contains the nimble flame . . .
every living thing is rooted in me.
Hildegaard of Bingen, The Book of Divine Words 4.11

Earth, as a result of human action, is now experiencing a monumental change. God is speaking to us through this. Our generation has been chosen by God to respond to the most momentous period of change in the billions of years of earth's history. The chemistry, bio-systems, geology and ozone layer are changing more radically than they ever have, and life systems are being extinguished at an unparalleled rate.

The disconnection with the natural world in the Western world and in the Western Church, in its thinking and worship patterns, cannot endure. In the East the Orthodox Ecumenical Patriarch Bartholomew has called for a radical raising of consciousness of the inter-dependence of the earth, humans and the world of the spirit. The rising Celtic spirituality in the West calls us to repentance for treating the earth like materialistic tyrants, and to re-enthrone life and worship as a sacrament of humility, thanksgiving and transformation until we become part of cosmic liturgy.

Thomas Berry, the Passionist priest and exponent of Creation Theology, speaks of a new cosmogony in which seven moments of grace in the evolution of the cosmos need to be celebrated. None of us would be here if it were not for the last explosion of a supernova some five billion years ago. Certain trace elements indispensable for our bodies' existence are only to be found as a result of such explosions. We are thus seen to be an intimate part of the whole universe. He writes, 'There are some 200 million indigenous (First World) people in the world. One of the first things we learn from these peoples is that the universe is a community of subjects, not a collection of objects.'

Celtic, like Orthodox spirituality, has never lost the sense of the unity of all creation in the praise of God and *The Celtic Prayer Book* is a means of restoring what has been lost. The patterns of worship in this section are contributions to this end.

Blessing the Earth

This may be held in the open air at midsummer
or any other time

Representatives bring a small bag of earth from their area

Thanksgiving

Leader	The earth is the Lord's
All	and everything in it.
Leader	Let all the people give God praise
All	and all creation bless God's name.

There may be singing

First   How precious is the soil the Lord has made.
It is rich and fertile; a single seed planted in it
will bring forth a hundred seeds.

Second   How beautiful is the soil the Lord has made.
Frail seeds blown by gentle winds become garlands
of colour flowering in crevice and cranny.

Third   How mysterious is the soil the Lord has made. Its
deeps bring forth minerals with which we bring
buildings, energy and ornament to our lives.

Fourth   How fruitful is the soil the Lord has made. It
brings forth crops of wheat and wood, of fruits
and nuts, of roots and berries.

Fifth   How hospitable is the soil the Lord has made.
Can the sheep and cows eat grass without the
soil? Even the birds who soar above the highest

mountain must return to earth to find food. The earth provides a bed for the ocean, and a floor for humankind.

Sixth   How like a mother is the soil the Lord has made. It contains us and feeds us, it warms us and upholds us.

All   God our Provider, bless our earth and bless us your people who live by it.

Psalm 148 may be read

Praise for the plants

The leader has a list of plants that are in the view or locality of those present. Some participants may be asked to bring a plant, or to add further examples. The leader invites everyone to raise a hand towards the sky. Those who wish to may name a plant

Leader   For *(name the plant)*
All   we bless you, generous Giver.
Any   For *(name the plant)*
All   we bless you, generous Giver . . .

Leader   High King of the universe, thank you for these plants your earth gives to us, and for all the blessings of life you shower upon us. In your goodness let the soil bring forth abundance and renew the joy of all your children on earth.

There may be singing or creative activity

Reader   Leviticus 25:1-12 or Isaiah 24:1-13

The earth blessing

The leader invites those who have brought bags of earth to pour the earth from them in to an earthen pot. The leader lays his/her hand on the earth

Leader   Nurturing God, bless this soil, the soil on which we live and work and make community. In your mercy may it bring forth goodness to nourish and renew the whole community who shares it.

Reader   You made the earth and through the long ages planted it with every kind of plant, and made animals to crawl and to run upon it, birds to fly over it, and fish to swim around it.

Groups with the necessary musical resources may play music that expresses the variety and abundance of this teeming life

Leader   When all was prepared, you formed humankind from the soil. You breathed your life into them. May we never forget that we are mortal creatures; from earth we come, to earth we go. We did not make ourselves. Indeed, we and the earth itself need to be redeemed through the Saviour who restored unity between earth and heaven. In the name of the One who came from heaven yet was born of earth, let us each bless the earth.

The leader invites each person, in a moment of recollection, to become tuned to their surroundings, to choose a spot or a living thing, and to lay a hand of blessing upon it, praying silently

God's Word

Reader   Matthew 21:33-41 or Matthew 6:25-30

There may be teaching or group work

Intercession

Leader   We offer you the earth and the vegetables
              that grow from it,
All   for all creation is yours
              and we want to be enriching it.

Leader   We offer you the earth and the minerals
              that lie under it,
All   for all creation is yours
              and we want to be enriching it.

Leader   We offer you the earth and the birds and beasts
              that move over it,
All   for all creation is yours
              and we want to be enriching it.

Leader   We offer you ourselves who make our home
              upon the earth,
All   for all creation is yours
              and we want to be enriching it.

A song to accompany the prayers

© Rev. Andrew Dick. Reproduced by kind permission.

There may be chanting of alleluias or other singing

Leader   Bless to us, O God,
the earth that is beneath us,
the sky that is above us,
your image deep within us,
the life that lies before us.

There may be feasting and celebration

Blessing of Animals and Toys

O God, I thank you for all the creatures you have made,
so perfect in their kind –
great animals like the elephant and the rhinoceros,
humorous animals like the camel and the monkey,
friendly ones like the dog and the cat,
working ones like the horse and the ox,
timid ones like the squirrel and the rabbit,
majestic ones like the lion and the tiger,
and for birds with their songs.
O God, give us such love for your creation
that love may cast out fear
and all your creatures see in a human being
their priest and friend.

George Appleton

Hear our humble prayer, O God, for our friends the animals,
especially the animals who are suffering;
for any that are hunted or lost,
deserted or frightened or hungry,
for all that must be put to death.
We entreat your pity for those who deal with them
and ask for a heart of compassion and gentle hands
and kindly words.
Make us ourselves to be true friends to animals
and so to share the blessings of the merciful.

Attributed to Albert Schweitzer

We pray for the humble beasts who with us
bear the burden and heat of the day,
giving their lives for the well-being of their countries;
and for the wild creatures, whom you have made wise,
strong and beautiful.
We ask for them your great tenderness of heart
for you have promised to save both man and beast,
and great is your loving kindness, O Saviour of the world.

From Russia

Brothers and sisters who supply our need of food,
may the blessing of the Divine Provider
who made you this way
be upon you and upon us as we gratefully eat,
that there may be peace between your spirit and ours.

May all beings regard me with the eye of a friend
and I all beings.

The whales sing and play all day
and so do the creatures nearer home.
May we learn from them to sing and play in our hearts
even when we have less important things to do.

Soft toys in church

Lord, these your little ones
bring their stuffed companions to this rail of blessing.
To us slow adults – stuffed, inanimate and something
they'll grow out of.
To them – the sacrament
that you lie down with them when they go to sleep;
that angels really do dwell with them;
that their tired eyes and weary limbs
from a day's thousand growing-up experiences
can rest with an unchanging form beside them,
unchanging except for the slow wearing away
of fur or wool by being loved.
Lord, bless these soft toys presented to you
for your affirmation today;
and make me more childlike
in trusting your power to bless
through things made indirectly in your image.
Bless Teddy, Owlie, Hippo, Dyno and all the others,
and especially bless those whom they bless.
And bring into your kingdom of love
countless thousands of your little ones,
love, joy and peace.

Ian Silk, Holy Island 1999

Celebrating Creation

All   You are the Rock from which all worlds
            are fashioned.
            You are the Food from which all souls are fed.
            You are the Force from which all power lines
            travel.
            You are the Source who is creation's head.

There may be singing

Leader We give you thanks for the great moments
            of grace in the evolution of the cosmos and for
            the healing story of our universe: for that
            moment when something came into being when
            before there was nothing; for exploding
            primeval atoms that brought galaxies to birth;
            for the compassionate curvature of space that
            sustained them; for the death of a star that
            brought to birth planet earth; for the emergence
            of the elements, earth and air, fire and water,
            and of life itself; for the coming into being of
            minerals, vegetables and creatures; for the co-
            operation, not just the competition, between all
            that live; for the human person, endowed with
            conscience, intelligence and mercy, a co-creator
            with you.

All   Glory to the Birther,
            glory to the Son,
            glory to the Spirit,
            making creation one.

Reader Psalm 104:24-30

Thanksgiving

Leader	We bless you, Lord,
All	for the beauty of the trees,
	the softness of the air and the fragrance of the grass.
Leader	We bless you, Lord,
All	for the soaring of the skies,
	the rhythms of the earth,
	the stillness of the night.
Leader	We bless you, Lord.
All	for the freshness of the morning,
	the dewdrops on the flower,
	the twinkling of the stars.
Leader	We bless you, Lord,
All	for the taste of good food,
	the trail of the sun and the life that never goes away.

Chief Dan George

God's Word

Reader Genesis 49:22-26 or Exodus 23:14-19

Reader Genesis chapters 1-11 encompass a movement from creation to civilisation. Although they tell the story of the alienation of humans from the rest of creation, and the curse their disobedience brought upon the land, there remains a moral continuity between humans and the land. Our relationship to the land is linked with its relationship to God and ours. Humans are to have dominion over the land as those who reflect God's likeness: that is, through love.

All	Holy, holy, holy perfect Lord of hosts,
	heaven and earth are full of your glory.
Reader	You have created all creatures with your word.
	You carry them all without being weary,
	and feed them all without ceasing.
All	You think about them all without forgetting any.
	You give to all without being diminished.
	You water all the earth without running dry.
Reader	You watch over all without sleeping.
	You hear us all without neglecting any.
	Although your presence fills every place,
	your messengers have told us about you
	in a way we can receive.

Ethiopian Orthodox Liturgy

Reader Luke 12:22-31 or Colossians 1:9-20

Proclamation

All We believe, O God of the cosmos,
that you are the eternal Maker of life.
We believe, O God of all gods,
that you are the eternal Maker of love.
We believe, O Lord and God of all people,
that you are the Creator of the skies above,
of the earth beneath, of the oceans below.
We believe, O Lord and God of all people,
that you are the One who created our bodies
from earth,
that you gave to our bodies their breath
and to our souls eternal worth.

or

Leader	These are the words of Yahweh,
	in whom the cosmos has its being:
All	I am in all things – the earth, the sky, the sea.
	I am in all seasons – the dark, the light, the shade.
	I am in all beings – the birds, the beasts
	and mortals.
	Wherever there is life – I AM.

There may be teaching, creative activity and singing

Question	What is best in this world?
Answer	To do the will of our Maker.
Question	What is his will?
Answer	That we should live according to the laws
	of his creation.
Question	How do we know those laws?
Answer	By study – studying the Scriptures with devotion.
Question	What tool has our Maker provided for this study?
Answer	The intellect which can probe everything.
Question	And what is the fruit of study?
Answer	To perceive the eternal Word of God reflected
	in every plant and insect, every bird and animal,
	and every man and woman.

This has been named as Ninian's Catechism

Intercession

Any of the following may be used

Leader	Creator and Saviour,
	we have exploited earth for our selfish ends,
	turned our backs on the cycles of life
	and forgotten we are your stewards.

Now soils become barren,
air and water become unclean,
species disappear,
and humans are diminished.
Forgive us and teach us to pray for your creation.

First Caring Father,
in you we live and move and have our being.
Sustain those who eke out the minerals,
create textures, grow crops or rear cattle.
Give us wisdom to manage technology
for the world's good.
Bless all work done today
that enables the human family
to be clothed, fed and housed in dignity,
receive a fair return for their work,
and celebrate the gift of life.

Second Dear Saviour,
who restored unity between earth and heaven,
teach us to care for your earth,
and to be good stewards of all that is in it.
May we learn how to live in harmony
with your laws.
Bless the soil on which we live and work
and make community.
May it bring forth goodness to nourish and renew
all who share it.

Third Great Spirit,
whose breath is felt in the soft breeze,
may we cherish the precious earth,
the earth of the God of life.

May we provide for those who can neither
sow nor reap
because human ills have drained them.

Fourth   As the sun circles the earth
circle the creation, O God.
Bless the earth that is beneath us,
the sky that is above us,
your image deep within us,
the day that lies before us.

Fifth   You who shaped the coastlines
and put healing sounds into the earth,
our hearts flow into your big heart
as small springs flow into the big sea.

There may be singing and creative activity

Leader   Dear planet earth,
the Light of all light shine on you,
the Power of all power energise you,
the Love of all love transform you.
Dear people,
the Love of all love transform you.

The First Day of Summer (Beltane)

In ancient Celtic tradition summer is known as Beltane. It begins on 1 May and ends on the last day of July. The official months of summer today are June to August in the northern hemisphere and December to February in the southern hemisphere.

The following celebration may take place in the setting of a meal or gathering in a home, church or public space

Introduction

First Farewell, season of sowing and hidden striving;
now toil will bear its fruit.
Beauty, once hidden,
will come forth like a bride.

Second Welcome, season of growth and friendship,
season of activity and celebration.
May ardour, vigour and chivalrous love
flow strongly in our veins;
may heroes and holy ones shine forth.

All A blessing on the season of growth,
on all that is done and felt:
the blessing of the fertile Creator,
the blessing of the virile Son,
the blessing of the Spirit, the sustaining One.

There may be music or singing

Thanksgiving

Leader Let us celebrate the work of the world:
All May desk and treetops praise you.
May lambs and new-made clothes praise you.
May fuel and transport praise you.

Leader Let us celebrate the renewal of nature:
All May its scents and sounds praise you.
May the growing trees praise you.
May the skies and the breeze praise you.

Leader Let us celebrate the joys of life:
All May lovers praise you, in love of the King of Life.
May gardens and sports praise you.
May swans and elegant music praise you.

Leader Let us celebrate the refreshments of life:
All May friendship and enterprise praise you.
May strength and the beauty of little things
praise you.
May ecstasy and mystery praise you.

Dedication

Leader At the start of Beltane, this fresh season,
we acknowledge your presence
in the mysterious shaping of our lives.
We dedicate to you our intentions,
our emotions, our deeds
and all that we touch.
We dedicate to you the earth
on which we shall make our life,
the people we shall work with.

	We dedicate to you all that we shall touch,
-------	the materials of this earth and all that breathes.
All	Christ be in the earth and each thing we touch.
	Christ be in the work and each thing we do.
	Christ be in the mind and each thing we pursue.

Leader   Let us kindle our souls
at the forge of nature's Soul-smith.
All   A spark of life to us.
A spark of light to us.
A spark of love to us.

There may be meditation or free prayer

Leader   As we enter this season of creativity
All   may we think your thoughts after you.

Leader   As we enter our beds of hope
All   may we dream your dreams after you.

Leader   As we explore new realms of life
All   may your life renew our being.

Early Crops

In early Celtic tradition earth's various harvests are celebrated over a three-month period. These begin with the first cereal crops on 1 August (later named Lammas), and end with the harvest of nuts and berries on 1 November (1 February to 1 May in the southern hemisphere). Since, before calendar changes, Lammas was eleven days earlier, and since new strains of seed for winter sowing have brought forward the first crops, these may be celebrated earlier.

This three-month period is a time to adore our life-giving God for these crops, and for the human activities and possibilities that grow out of them. It is a time to hold the material universe in awe, respect and gratitude, and also the tools with which we fashion it.

Households or churches may invite neighbours to a garden celebration at the time of the early crops.

Lammas refers to the loaf made from the first ripe corn. Traditionally, on 1 August a loaf would be baked from flour made from the first wheat to be harvested. It would be baked on either an open-air or a household fire, around which circling prayers would be sung.

Morning or Evening Prayer for Early Crops

A loaf is cooked from freshly produced flour or a barbecue with freshly made rolls is arranged

Leader   Following the growth of sunlit days
All   let us bless the first of the crops.

Leader	We offer you the first of our crops
	and the best of our lives –
All	all that we have, all that we are,
	all that we will ever be.
Leader	For all things come from you, and of your own
	do we give you.
All	Yours is the life and the power and the glory of all.

There may be singing

God's Word

Reader Exodus 23:14-19

There may be silence

Thanksgiving

Light

First reader lights a candle

First I bring light to offer God in thanksgiving.
Without light no living thing would survive.
Without light all things would perish.

All Fire and heat, bless the Lord.
Sun and moon, bless the Lord.
Light and energy, bless the Lord.

First We bless you, Giver of light.
We bless you, Provider of warmth.
We bless you, Disperser of darkness.

270

Water

The second reader brings a glass of water

Second I bring water in thanksgiving.
Without water the plants would perish.
Without water the earth would become a desert.

All Rain and reservoirs, bless the Lord.
Springs and streams, bless the Lord.
Seas and flood plains, bless the Lord.

Second We bless you, Giver of water.
We bless you, Sender of dew and rain.
We bless you, Refresher of the parched soil.

Air

The third reader waves a streamer, sprig or branch

Third I bring air to offer to God in thanksgiving.
Without air we would die very quickly.
Without air no living creature could survive.

All Winds of God, bless the Lord.
Gentle breezes, bless the Lord.
Mighty gales, bless the Lord.

Third We bless you, Breath of life.
We bless you, Sustainer of our world.
We bless you, the Spirit who renews our being.

*Representatives of local business and workplaces
may bring samples of their products*

There may be teaching and singing

Bread

The leader holds up the loaf of bread

Leader   I bring a loaf and offer this to God
on behalf of us all.

Fourth   Be gentle when you touch bread.
Let it not lie, uncared for, unwanted.
So often bread is taken for granted.
There is such beauty in bread –
beauty of sun and soil,
beauty of patient toil.
Wind and rain have caressed it,
Christ often blessed it.
Be gentle when you touch it.

Anon

Leader   O God, who put ear in corn, and skill and love
in human hands that make and hold this bread,

All   you are the Rock from which all earth is fashioned;
you are the Food from which all souls are fed.

Leader   Great God, who gave birth to the universe,
be born again in us.
As the grains of wheat were scattered on a
thousand fields and now become one in this
loaf, so may we, who are scattered in a thousand
places, become one Body in Christ.

*The loaf is passed round and each person breaks
off a piece and eats it*

*There may be teaching, singing, music, circling,
eating, dancing, festivity*

Lament

Leader We confess that in our blest world
we are so ungrateful.

All sing Kyrie Eleison *(x 3) or say* God, have mercy.

Leader We confess that in our bountiful world
so many are hungry.

All sing Kyrie Eleison *(x 3) or say* God, have mercy.

Leader We confess that in our beautiful world
so much is being destroyed.

All sing Kyrie Eleison *(x 3) or say* God, have mercy.

Leader May the grains be wholesome, and not be signs
of the poisoning of soil and rivers.
May the womb which bears the world's water
not be violated by mindless human action.
May we sustain the conditions for a well-watered
world that brings well-being to us and our children.

Reader Jesus said: Happy are those who are humble,
for they shall inherit the earth.

Matthew 5:5

There may be singing

Intercessions

Reader We pray for:
flour mills, combine harvesters and individuals
who harvest by hand;
heavy goods vehicles delivering the flour
and bread to the shops;
shops that stock and sell these good things
of the earth;

kitchens and homes that they may be signs
of blessing;
those who eke out a living in parched
or flooded lands.

The leader, followed by any person, may bring a candle, light it and place it on the table as a prayer for a part of the world denied the harvest and fullness of life that we enjoy.

> *This prayer may be silent or spoken aloud. After each prayer or candle placing all may sing or say a response such as 'O Lord, hear my prayer'*

Leader   We give you back the months that are past.
We offer our best for what is to come.

Leader   The sheaves and the green leaves fall.
All   Generous be our hearts,
open be our hands,
justice be our benchmark,
thanksgiving be our call.

Leader   For the sake of your great giving,
O Christ, who was ground like flour,
our Bread of Life,
feed and nourish us evermore.

Night Prayer for Early Crops

Leader   Summer ripens;
first crops are gathered.
All   It is time to gather our thoughts.
Leader   Blessings are stored;
gratitude is ours.

All	It is time to be generous of heart.
Leader	Our first fruit of this season,
	the sign of our love,
All	is to give you, as homage, our all.

There may be singing

Reader   Psalm 90:1-4; 10-12

A loaf is placed on a table
A reader holds it up and says:

Reader   There is such beauty in bread –
beauty of sun and soil,
beauty of patient toil.
Wind and rain have caressed it,
Christ often blessed it.
Be gentle when you touch it.

Anon

Reader   Creator of the earth,
Keeper of our memories,
give us wisdom to harvest our life
and find the wholeness of memory.

All   Heal our wounds,
keep bright the flame.
Kindle in us
the memory of love and discovery,
the memory of daring and longing.

Leader   We bring to you also our distant memories
of abandoned areas of our lives. Tonight we
invite you to come close to us and heal these.

Silent reflection

Leader	Visit these places with compassion, O Lord, in this ripening season. Shine your kindly and forgiving rays of understanding upon them until the eternal light and beauty that is within us meet them and bring freedom to our spirits.

There may be singing or sharing

Reader	Mark 4:26-29
Leader	Now let us gather before God the names of those we carry in our hearts.

Any may mention names; any that have been put in a book or box may be read out

There may be singing

Leader	The seed is Christ's, the granary is Christ's.
All	In the granary of God may we be gathered.
Leader	The sea is Christ's, the fishes are Christ's.
All	In the nets of God may we all meet.

St Martin Wine Blessing

An ancient Christian custom is to bless the life and work of an area. In agricultural areas people may walk with tractors, stop where there are different crops and ask blessing on the seeds that have been planted. In industrial areas people may walk with an open-top bus or a car trailer, blessing different kinds of commerce, industry or leisure activity. Here is an example of an ancient prayer of blessing which can be adapted to the situation:

O Monarch of the Tree of Life,
may the blossoms bring forth the sweetest fruit,
may the birds sing out the highest praise,
may your Spirit's gentle breath cover all.

This pattern of worship may be used to celebrate the season of new wine or the patron saint of wine makers, Martin of Tours, who died on 11 November 397. More generally, the vineyard may be used as a symbol of the healing of the land, as it is in Scripture.

Welcome

There may be a welcome and singing

Reader   Isaiah 25:1, 6

Leader   Jesus said: I am the true vine.
All   Your life becomes our life.

Leader   I am the bread of life.
All   You feed and fill the hungry.

| Leader | I am the way, the truth and the life. |
| All | You renew the face of the earth. |

There may be singing or Psalm 80 may be read

Seeking forgiveness

| Leader | Jesus says: 'Every branch that bears fruit, my Father, who is the vine grower, prunes to make it bear more fruit.' (Pruning lays the foundation upon which the crop and its wine quality depends.) |
| All | Lord, we are sorry for our failure to love and cherish your creation and your children; we are sorry for the neglect and misuse which have violated what you intend for them. |

All may say or sing:

Mercy, Lord; mercy, Lord; have mercy, Lord; have mercy, Lord.

Blessing the vines

| Leader | God of life, you are the giver of growth, the refresher of earth, and you delight in the joys of human celebration: in this new season bless the vines and the wine making; bless those who make their livelihood from it, and those whose tables shall be enriched by it. |
| First | Ever loving God, you called Martin from military service to be a hermit and a shepherd in your Church. May we, following his example |

of care for the earth and its needy, deal gently
with all people, that we and the earth may be
clothed in righteousness, through Jesus Christ,
earth's Redeemer.

Second   Lord of the Church,
look with mercy on this your vineyard.
Where it is in danger, guard it;
where it goes astray, prune it;
where its growth is stunted, nourish it;
and where it strikes true, strengthen it.

All   Amen.

There may be singing and celebration

Last Ingathering of Crops

A Household or Church Candle-lighting

This is a time of both physical and spiritual garnering, a time for remembering, a time to celebrate the lives of those who have established noble values, exercised wise judgement, and steered others towards fullness of light. (See Volume One – Remembrance.) Every aspect of this 'gathering in' is prayed for and blessed.

The household table may be decorated with berries, nuts or fruits arranged around a candle

First This is the time when the last crops are gathered in, the harvest of nuts and berries and ripening fruit.

All May it be for us a season of ripening understanding,
a season of nourishment and deepening love
that brings healing to our lives.

A candle is lit

Second There are seasons of the heart;
there is a season to take stock of blessings,
to gather in the fragments of memory,
to store up good things
from which to feed upon in the years ahead,
to become generous in sharing.

Third Autumn (the Fall) is a wonderful time
to develop the art of inner harvesting.
There is a beauty to the inner harvest.

By gathering together the fragments
we get to know our story.
Only when we know our story
are we whole people.

Fourth   A new strength and poise and belonging comes
that was never available to us
when we spent all our days
rushing distractedly around.
This is a season to come home
to our deeper nature.

All   Gather together the fragments of our lives
and bring us to the place of fulfilment
where we are held by you.

Prayer for the Winter Solstice

In the Northern Hemisphere this is 21 December.

This may be used as a normal Night Prayer or as the framework for an outdoor celebration as follows. People gather round a fire in an open place after dark. Hot food, drink and music may be provided at a nearby building which may be decorated with holly, mistletoe or local greenery. Mistletoe is considered to be a sacred plant. Its white symbolises the energy of the sun. Another name for it is 'heal-well'. Some may choose to stay up until the early hours, enjoying the sights and sounds of the night.

Leader   Come, Creator of lights, pierce the darkness
and light up the earth.
Light up the seas, light up the lonely and the sad.

First or females

Christ at the yearly turning,
Christ at every bend,
Christ at each beginning,
Christ at every end.

Second or males

Christ in dark's deep shadows,
Christ in shades of death,
Christ in primeval history,
Christ in wintry earth.

Reader   Psalm 139:1-12

There may be singing that reflects the mystery of God and of creation or the following Taizé chant may be repeated:

All	Within our darkest night
	you kindle the fire that never dies away,
	that never dies away. *(x 2)*

First   Craftsperson of the heavens, you have stretched out above us a canopy of stars which are signs of hope renewed in darkest times.

Second   Brightener of the night, open to us the treasures of darkness – its deepest wisdom and its healing power.

Males	The world is not dead;
Females	it is sleeping.
Males	Its life draws in;
Females	it is keeping.
Males	The earth is gathering energy
Females	for a new burst of life.
Males	We breathe in the mystic air
Females	that we may breathe out care.
Males	Your presence supports us through the night
Females	so we can hail the coming source of Light.
Males	Shine through the mists, the deadening heavy clod.
All	Hail gladdening Light of God's pure glory poured,
	Holiest of holies, Jesus Christ our Lord.

There may be singing or a pause

Leader   Tonight God's Presence is shrouded in mystery. Awe and respect are restored to their rightful place.

Reader   Do not be deceived. Every good gift comes from God, the Creator of the lights of the heavens. Darkness is not caused by any unreliability in God.

James 1:16-18

Leader   Lord of the seasons, on this day of briefest light
help us to be at home with the treasures of the
dark.

*There may be a pause, or anyone may mention
examples of these treasures*

Leader   As the days have drawn in, draw near to us
with your everlasting light.

*There may be a pause, or anyone may mention
examples of God's light*

Leader   As shadows lengthen, help us to embrace
the shadow of life.

*There may be a pause, or anyone may mention
examples of these*

Leader   As the dark swallows up the created sun, help us
to store up riches for the long days ahead.

Reader   'Listen!' says Jesus. 'I am coming soon! I
will bring my rewards with me, to give each
according to what they have done. I am the
first and the last, the beginning and the end . . .
I am descended from the family of David.
I am the bright morning star . . .

Verses from Revelation 22:12-16

Creative activities for an open-air celebration

There may be warming drinks following the above reading

There may be singing, dancing or music-making

Following this each person may go to an open-air space where they try and sense the mystery of the dark, the rhythm of the seasons, the energy of the earth, the glory of the elements.

It may be possible to touch a tree and feel its breathing; to feel the flow of life beginning to move in the earth. Listen to what is there.

Reach out to welcome all that it is to bring forth.

Bless the four elements in turn: the earth, the air, the fire, the water. When you are ready, return to the fire and the food.

There may be dancing in a circle to mirror the circle of the coming sun. Before people begin to go home, everyone holds hands in a circle, walks in the direction of the sun (east to west) and prays the circling prayer below together.

Reader	Circle me, Lord;
All	keep light within,
	keep demons without.
Reader	Circle me, Lord;
All	keep hope within,
	keep despair without.
Reader	Circle me, Lord;
All	keep trust within,
	keep fear without.

Leader   Circle your world, Lord, and circle those we love
Any   (*names may be mentioned*)

Leader   In the chill depths of winter send fire from
heaven to all who have grown cold in their
hearts. May the glowing saints and angels bring
them life fires from the heart of God.

We lie down tonight
under the warming of the Father,
we lie down tonight
under the kindling of the Son,
we lie down tonight
under the glowing of the Spirit,
ever Three and ever One.

Night Prayer for New and Full Moons

Leader Many a soul has passed beyond
in the time between the two moons,
but we are still enjoying earth
in the gleam of the moon above.

Leader Creator of moons,
Saving Light,
Sheen-bright Spirit . . .

either (for new moon)

Leader tonight your glory shines among us anew.
All We welcome your Presence, renewing itself
in our midst.

or (for full moon)

Leader tonight your glory shines in its fullness.
All May we receive of your fullness tonight.

Leader We praise you for creating sun, moon and stars
All and for revealing your glory to us.
Leader You have assigned them tasks
which they perform without demur;
All may we perform willingly in the orbit of your love.

*An arm of the reader or of everyone may be raised
to salute the moon*

Reader   Moon of gentle light,
guiding jewel of the night,
we raise our hand to you,
we lift our eye to you.
You are travelling your course,
you blessing of God,
you moon that graces the seasons.

Reader   Psalm 8 or 81

Leader   God is the beauty within everything
that has been created.
In the twilight may that beauty shine out
and become the divine Presence,
encompassed in the mystery of the gloaming.

All   When the two worlds embrace and are at peace –
the dark and the light,
the day and the night,
the strong and the tender –
then we may rest in peace.

There may be silence or sharing

Reader   May the Moon of moons
be coming through thick clouds
on me and on every one;
coming through dark tears,
coming on me as I sleep,
and coming on those we love.

Leader   Our dear ones bless, O God, in every place
where they are.

Any   (*may name loved ones or needy people and places*)

This prayer is said for all who have been named:

All   Grace of wellbeing be yours.
          Grace of the love of the stars be yours.
          Grace of the love of the moon be yours.
          Grace of the God of the night.

Reader   Colossians 1:17-20

          There may be singing

Leader   May the Moon of moons rest upon us now.
          Holy be each thing she bathes.
          Holy be each person she illumines
All   We lie down bathed in your light.

Leader   As we go to our rest 'neath the sheen of grace
          in the time between two gloamings,
          may we sleep in the gentle light of heaven
          and wake to pursue our course.

New Year's Night

This is largely based on a Jewish form of prayer

Leader   Blest are you, King of the ages.
You set the stars in their courses.
You cause times and seasons to change.
You have brought us to another year.
You make the day to fade and bring on the night.

All   Blest are you, Lord of the years.

Leader   You have loved your people with everlasting love.
You have taught us truth and duty and justice.
We will lie down with these and waking,
live by them.

All   Blest are you Lord, Lord of the years.

Leader   Blest are you who love your people by day
and by night.
Blest are you who have brought us to another year.

All   You are the Lord our God who is One.

There may be singing

Reader   Love the Lord your God with all your heart, and all
your soul, and all your strength. These words that I
command you today shall be upon your heart.
Repeat them to your children, and talk about
them when you sit in your home,
and when you walk in the street;
when you lie down, and when you rise up.
Hold fast to them as a sign upon your hand,
and let them be reminders before your eyes.

Deuteronomy 6:4-9

| **Leader** | The Lord our God, and no other, exists. |
| **All** | The Lord shall rule for ever. |

Leader	Father, help us to lie down in peace
	and to rise up in your life.
	Spread over us a covering of peace.
	Give us counsel in the night.
	Shield us from enemy, loss and harm.
	Shelter us under the shadow of your wings.

| **All** | We bless the Lord by night. |
| | We bless the Lord when we lie down. |

Leader	In your hands are the souls of the living
	and the dead,
	of every creature and every mortal.
	We remember before you those whom we love
	and those in special need.

There may be silence or names may be mentioned

There may be the creative activity and singing

Leader	Into your hands we place our beings,
	for you have redeemed us, Lord God of truth.
	Rule in us for ever.
All	Lead us to the heritage you have prepared for us.

PRAYER RHYTHMS
FOR THE
NATURAL SEASONS

Spring (or Imbolc)

Spring is the first season of the year, in which vegetation begins to appear. In the northern hemisphere it starts between March and May and in the southern hemisphere between September and October. In Celtic tradition, Imbolc (the weeks between 1 February and 30 April) is the spring season. It marks the end of winter and the returning of the light; it is a time of beginnings, fresh inspiration, and planning for growth; a time to celebrate gestating life in the worlds of nature and the Spirit.

Spring Candle-lighting

*The spring candle-lighting may precede any meal or
worship-gathering during spring
The patterns of worship that follow may be used on a Sunday
or on a public holiday any time during the three months
of spring*

Leader   Glorious Source, we give you greeting!
Let Sister Earth and Brother Sun praise you.
Let the fields and the forests praise you.
Let the birds and the beasts praise you.
Let everything that has breath praise you,
Mother and Father of all that has being.

Reader   Sacred One, look at our brokenness.
We know that in all creation only the human
family has strayed from the Sacred Way.

Sacred One, teach us compassion and honour,
so that we may heal the earth
and heal one another.

The central candle is lit

Leader   Earth, in which lies seas and life-giving waters;
in which grow seeds, and on which fields
and food have come to be –
may she bestow to us the finest of her yield.
Earth, whose waters, common to all,
flow faithfully through the nights and days –
may she pour on us the milk of kindness
that brings us lustre.

*The first reader lights the candle, takes hold of a
black ribbon, faces the people and says:*

Reader   In the womb of darkness all life is conceived:
the blackness of space gave stars their birth;
from a star's death was born our earth;
out of earth's buried depths were born our
mountains and valleys.

All   By the word of the Lord were the heavens made;
all the host of them by the breath of God's mouth.

*The second reader lights a candle and takes
a green ribbon*

Reader   For Yahweh your God is bringing you
to a good land.

All   God's goodness fills all creatures.

*The third reader lights a candle and takes
a blue ribbon*

Reader   And God said, 'Let the waters bring forth
abundance of life.'

All   Most Sacred One,
may your living waters fill us to overflowing.
Make us as a floodplain of compassion.

*The fourth reader lights a candle and takes
a red ribbon*

Reader   Sunrise calls us to rise with the Sun of suns
to see as our ancestors have seen and summons
us, living and dead, to praise the living God.

All   Creator of light,
at the rising of your sun we rise to greet you
and meet you,
and to reflect your light on earth.

*The fifth reader lights a candle and takes
a yellow ribbon*

Reader   Whatever we do to the land we do to ourselves.
All   We affirm the worth of all creation.
We renounce the compulsion to dominate.

Leader   May the road rise to meet you.
May the wind be at your back.
May the sun shine on your labours.
May the soft rains fall on your fields
of endeavour.

Celtic prayer, adapted

Morning Prayer for Spring

Leader   Spring, with her colour, warmth, and scent;
season of budding, rebirth, intent.
Year by year God sends the spring;
promise and pardon mingling.
While Christ eternal from the cross,
bounty bestows from utter loss.

Reader   The broken, cold, and stagnant earth
awakes with miracles of birth,
and spirits, broken, contrite, cold,
are healed with blessings manifold.
Beauty is free to walk abroad
and spread the glory of the Lord.

Peter Howard

There may be singing

Reader   Psalm 104:24-30

Leader   Christ comes to renew the face of the earth.
All   Let all creation rise to greet its returning
Splendour.

Reader   We arise today in the energy of the fertile earth.
We arise today in the promise of the rising seed.
We arise today in the goodness of the greening
leaves.

There may be a creative activity or a reading

God's Word

Reader   Genesis 1:24-31a *or another Old Testament reading*

Leader   Fresh shoots and buds of promise,
All   be glad for the God of life.

Leader   First winged arrivals and ears of corn,
All   be glad for the God of life.

Leader   Frolicking lambs and industrious bees,
All   be glad for the God of life.

There may be singing

Reader   Mark 4:26-28 *or another New Testament reading*

Thanksgiving

Leader   Spring and sunshine, praise your God.
All   Fresh shoots and buds, bless the Giver of life.

Leader   Earth and sky, praise your God.
All   All that swims in the sea, bless the Giver of life.

Leader   Soil and seeds, praise your God.
All   Hedgerows and lambs, bless the Giver of life.

Leader   Days of light, praise your God.
All   Returning life, bless the Giver of life.

Leader   Birds that sing, praise your God.
All   People in love, bless the Giver of life.

There may be a creed, teaching, creative activity or singing

Intercession

Leader   Glad Bringer of brightness,
spring's blessing, rainbow's embrace,
teach our hearts to open as the buds open
and to welcome in your grace.
Teach us to dance with the playful clouds
and to laugh with the sun's smile on our face.
The earth is yours; may it bring forth its produce.
The birds are yours; may they bring forth
their songs.
Our work is yours; may it bring forth its yield.

Reader   The face of nature laughs in the springtime;
All   restore laughter to our lives.

Reader   Her breath is fresh, and her eyes are clearest blue;
All   restore freshness to our lives.

Reader   The call of the birds is wild and free;
All   restore lightness to our lives.

Reader   Waterfalls splash with joy;
All   restore joy to our lives.

Reader   Meadows light up with the colours of flowers;
All   restore colour to our lives.

Reader   The breeze is nature's harp, playing a song of love;
All   restore love-songs to our lives.

Reader   People grow strong and beautiful
and the world is in love with its Creator;
All   restore strength and beauty to our lives.

There may be free prayer and singing

Reader I will go forth to sow my seeds
in the name of God whose growth it needs,
and every seed that lies
beneath cold winter's eyes
shall take root in God's way.
Kissed by the winds that lightly run,
the new shoots shall leap to greet the sun.

Leader And may the blessing of the earth be on you,
the great round earth.
May you ever have a kindly greeting
for people you pass as you go along the roads.
And now may the Lord bless you,
and bless you kindly.

An old Irish blessing

Midday Prayer for Spring

Reader   After stagnant days,
            things begin to stir.
            All things grow.
            Green shoots appear.
            Buds open.
            And would I be dumb?

Reader   Psalm 148

Leader   In the middle of the day,
            may I be grounded, like the earth;
            may I be real, like the elements;
            may I be true, like the fire;
            may I be free, like the wind;
            may the love that is within me flow, like water;
            and may I not forget the flowers.
            Dear God, give me fragrance
            in my relationships.

            There may be singing or creative activity

Reader   Look how the wild flowers grow.
            They neither work
            nor make clothes for themselves.
            Yet not even King Solomon,
            with all his wealth,
            had clothes as beautiful
            as one of these flowers.

                        Matthew 6:28b-29

Reader   O Christ, my King,
for this fair earth which is my home awhile,
I bow my knee;
for quickening dawns, for still noons,
for laughter in children and love in lovers' eyes.
Every sight and sound is a voice that tells of you:
the rain is your tears
whenever I wound your image of me,
the sun is the shining of your face
at every victory.
Manifold are the joys of spring.

Bring forth warmth and brightness,
welcome newborn life,
bring innocence and trust to birth,
bring buds of love to bloom.

Midwife of Wisdom,
reveal to me the treasures of your heart,
open to me the secrets of life,
release in me the energies of growth.

There may be free prayer and the Lord's Prayer

Leader   God bless the earth that is beneath us,
the growth that is around us,
the spring that is before us,
your image deep within us.

Evening Prayer for Spring

Leader   Glad Bringer of Brightness,
we come to bless you.

There may be singing or a creative activity

Reader   Psalm 104:1, 10-24

Leader   Hail to you, glorious Lord:
All   may the green of spring praise you,
may buds and blossom praise you,
may the shrub and fruit-tree praise you.
Leader   Abraham praised you, the founder of faith:
All   may the birds and the bees praise you,
may the stubble and the grass praise you,
may the bursting new life praise you.
Leader   Aaron and Moses praised you:
may male and female praise you,
may the seven days and the stars praise you,
may all the good things created praise you.
All   We, too, shall praise you, glorious Lord
of earth and heaven.

*There may be singing or a creative activity
using signs of spring*

Reader   Isaiah 40:28-31 *or another Old Testament reading*

Leader   We believe, O God of all gods,
that you are the eternal Maker of life.
We believe, O God of all gods,
that you are the eternal Maker of love.

All   We believe, O Lord and God of all people,
that you are the Creator of the high heaven,
that you are the Creator of the skies above,
that you are the Creator of the oceans below.

Leader   We believe, O Lord and God of all people,
that you are the One who created our souls
and set their course,
that you are the One who created our bodies
from earth,
that you gave to our bodies their breath
and to our souls their possession.

All   God, bless to us our bodies.
God, bless to us our souls.
God, bless to us our living.
God, bless to us our goals.

Reader   Colossians 1:9-20 *or another New Testament
reading. There may be silence*

First   Creator of the germ in woman,
Maker of seed in man,
giving life to the child in the body of its mother –
nursing it even in the womb,
soothing it that it may not weep –
Giver of breath to animate every one
whom you create:

Second   when the child comes forth from the womb
on the day of its birth,
you open its mouth in speech,
you supply its needs.

First   When the fledgling in the egg
            chirps in the shell,
            you give it breath to sustain its life.

All   How manifold are your works, O God!
            They are often hidden from us.
            Only God, whose power no other possesses,
            you created the earth according to your heart.

Echoes a prayer of Ikhnaton,
fourteenth century BC

There may be music, movement, storytelling,
poetry or singing

Leader Bringer of light and laughter,
            gifts of life are returning.
            Quicken our hearts within us.
            Release the beauty hidden within.

Reader Birther,
            bless the seeds and make them fertile,
            bless our thoughts and make them fruitful,
            bless wasted places and make them flourish.

            Life-giver,
            bring buds to flower,
            bring rain to the earth,
            bring songs to our hearts.

            Renewer,
            may fields become green,
            may beauty emerge,
            may dreams come to pass.

There may be free prayer

Leader   May the blessing of the rain be on us,
the sweet soft rain.
May it fall upon our spirits
so that all the little flowers may spring up
and shed their sweetness on the air.
May the blessing of the great rains be upon us
so that they beat upon our spirits
and wash them fair and clean
and leave there many a shining pool
where the blue of heaven shines,
and sometimes a star.

All   Thanks be to God.

Night Prayer for Spring

Leader   The face of nature laughs in springtime;
All   O God of life, smile on us tonight.

Leader   Nature's breath and eyes are clearest blue;
All   O purest God, gaze on us this night.

Reader   The blackbird's call is wild and free,
             rejoicing at the new abundance of food.
All   May our spirits become free this night,
             rejoicing in your abundance.

Reader   The meadows are alight with the colours
             of flowers in bloom;
All   may the colours of day make bright our dreams.

Reader   The sun glints through the fresh, green leaves;
All   may you gleam through the shades of our night.

Reader   The whole world is in love with its Creator;
All   may we lie down in love of you.

            There may be singing

Reader   Jesus said:
             The soil itself makes the plants grow
             and bear fruit;
             first the tender stalk appears,
             then the ear,
             and finally the full head.
                              Mark 4:28

Leader   If you were busy as we are, dear God,
             you would have no time for the slow wonder
             of spring's growth.

If you were busy as we are, dear God,
you would have no time to listen to us.
So we praise you for having time for all things,
and space to listen to us as we are silent before you.

Silence is kept

Leader   Each gift of spring I have received,
from you it came.
Each thing for which I hope, from your love
it will come.
Each fresh joy of life, it is of your bounty.

All sing

The King of love my shepherd is,
who rests me in green pastures,
who by still waters leads me on,
restores my soul for ever.

You make a feast for me to eat;
my life indeed is blessed.
Goodness befriends me all my days.
I'll live with you for ever.

Echoes Psalm 23

Leader   This night, bring the unopened buds in our life
into bloom:
Reader   Bring the searching for justice into bloom;
bring warmth and compassion into bloom;
Leader   in silence or aloud,
for ourselves or for others,
let us name things that need to come into bloom.

Leader Creator Spirit,
          wellspring of life and love, as we sleep:
All   renew the springs of our life,
          refresh our weak frame,
          restore love into our soul.
Leader God of springtime,
          renew us while sleeping,
          guide us when waking;
All   that awake we may watch with Christ
          and asleep we may rest in peace.

Creative Activities for Spring

1. Everyone (or just the children) is given a bulb to plant outside or at home.

2. Altars or focal points are decorated with plants and feathers, and spring flowers are displayed.

3. A spring theme corner is created.

4. Paint hard-boiled eggs and place these in a bowl.

Summer

In Celtic tradition the summer quarter of Beltane extends between 1 May and 31 July. It is a time of warmth and growth, of increased confidence and sociability. It is a time, also, to celebrate the vitality of life, the joys of youth, the adventures of heroes, the provisions of earth, the fullness of life and the goodness of God. The summer is also a good time to bless the earth.

Morning Prayer for Summer

Leader   These are the long days
when the sun rides high above us;
days we enjoy with you, our sustaining God.

Thanksgiving

Reader   Gratitude for the sun: blinding pulsing light,
through trunks of trees, through mists,
through walls,
warming caves and corridors –
the one who wakes us –
in our minds so be it.

Echoes a Mohawk prayer

Leader   The sun rises daily only because you command it.
Its splendour will not last,
created things all perish.

All   Christ, the true Sun nothing can destroy;
the Sun of suns, he shall reign for ever.

There may be singing

Reader   Psalm 104:1-14 *or* 148

Leader   The beauty of summer,
its days long and slow,

All   beautiful, too, visiting the ones we love.

Leader   The beauty of flowers
on the tops of fruit-trees,

All   beautiful, too, covenant with the Creator.

Leader	We rejoice in the energies of the sun; in the abundance that can be ours. Let each raise a hand to bless the sun and the earth and say together:
All	For the sun, and the blessings that flow from it, for the the earth and all it brings forth, we praise you, generous Giver.

There may be a short silence or blessings of summer may be named

God's Word

Reader	Job 38:1-15
Leader	We thank you, O God, for these amazing days, for the leaping greenery and the arching blue sky. Everything that breathes seems to cry, 'Yes!' Today, may our whole being cry 'Yes' to you.
First	Life of Jesus, Sun of suns, filling every part of us, life be in our speech, sense in what we say, the bloom of cherries on our cheeks, till you come back again.
Second	Love of Jesus, Sun of suns, filling every heart for us, love be in our deeds, strength in our frame traversing sea and air and field, rays of Jesus being our shield.
Reader	Matthew 6:25-33

All sing

All creatures of our God and King,
lift up your voice and with us sing
Hallelujah! Hallelujah!
You burning sun with golden gleam,
warming the earth with friendly beam,
we praise you, we praise you.
Hallelujah! Hallelujah! Hallelujah!
All you who come with grateful heart,
forgiving others, take your part,
praise your Maker. Hallelujah!
You who long pain and sorrow bear,
cast on your God your every care.
We praise you, we praise you.
Hallelujah! Hallelujah! Hallelujah!

Let all things their Creator bless,
and worship God in humbleness.
We praise you. Hallelujah!
Praise, praise the Father, praise the Son,
and praise the Spirit, Three in One.
We praise you, we praise you.
Hallelujah! Hallelujah! Hallelujah!

Based on Canticle of the Sun,
Francis of Assisi

Leader Jesus said: I came in order that you may have
life – life in all its fullness.

John 10:10

Our energies are strong, O God;
we have fullness of life in you.

Males   Sun shines,
              sap rises,
              buds burst.

Females   Lambs frolic,
              birds sing,
              people play.

All   Glory to God who sustains and nurtures us all.

Leader   May our eyes be open to see your hand in nature.

All   May our hands be open to cherish your gifts.
              May our hearts be open to love you in others.

Leader   May God's face smile upon us.
              May God's grace rain upon us.
              May God's blessing go with us.

All   We will go to bless God's world.

Midday Prayer for Summer

Leader   Rejoice you earth of sunlit days,
pointing us to Christ the true Sun
who lit up the world below
and then resplendent rose again.
Rejoice all spirits:
the ascending sun shines alike on the dead
and on the living;
as the true helios,
he climbed the heights of heaven;
Christ, the Sun of suns, scatters the darkness
from our path.
Rejoice, O earth, in shining splendour,
radiant in the brightness of your King!
Christ has conquered death!
Glory fills you!
Darkness vanishes for ever!

All   Alleluia!

Traditional Liturgy

Leader   Spilled on this earth are all the joys of heaven.

Joys may be named

Leader   You made the earth
and through the long ages planted it
with every kind of plant;
you made animals to crawl and to run upon it,
birds to fly over it,
and fish to swim around it.
When all was prepared, you formed humankind
from the soil.

You breathed your life into them.
You made the sun to shine upon them all.

All   We bless you for sun and for summer days.

There may be silence

Reader Jesus said: God makes the sun shine
on good and bad people alike.

Matthew 5:45

I am the Light of the world.
Whoever follows me will have the light of life
and will never walk in darkness.

John 8:12

Reader As the hand is made for holding
and the eyes for seeing,
you have fashioned me for joy.
Grant me your vision
that I may find it everywhere –
in the sunlit faces of our world,
in the wild flower's beauty,
in the lark's melody,
in a child's smile,
in a mother's love,
in the face of a steadfast man.

Free prayer or singing

Leader God bless the sun that is above us,
the earth that is beneath us,
the work that lies before us,
your image deep within us.

Evening Prayer for Summer

Leader   The earth is the Lord's
All   and everything in it.
Leader   Let all the people give God praise
All   and all creation bless God's name.

Reader   God of the longest day,
            may my life be a long day for you,
            always reflecting your light;
            open,
            awake.

Thanksgiving

There may be singing

Reader   Psalm 8

Leader   May summer and sunshine praise you.
All   May plain and hillside praise you.
Leader   May wind and blossom praise you.
All   May the cedar and sweet fruit tree praise you.
Leader   Abraham praised you, the founder of faith.
All   May life everlasting praise you.
Leader   May the birds and the bees praise you.
All   May the stubble and the grass praise you.
Leader   Aaron and Moses praised you.
All   May male and female praise you.
Leader   May the seven days and the stars praise you.
All   May books and letters praise you.
Leader   May the fish in the river praise you.
All   May thought and action praise you.

Leader	May the sand and the earth praise you.
All	May all the good things created praise you.
Leader	And I, too, shall praise you, King of glory.
All	Hail, glorious King!

Early Middle Welsh, adapted

God's Word

Reader	Deuteronomy 11:13-21, Isaiah 55:10-13 *or another Old Testament reading.*

Leader	For the rain forests gone, and the deserts caused by human destruction
All	we grieve with you, O Lord.
Leader	For polluted seas, dirty streets, and litter
All	we grieve with you, O Lord.
Leader	For not being content to savour the simple gifts of creation
All	we grieve with you, O Lord.

Reader	Mark 13:28-31; John 21:1-15 *or another New Testament reading*

There may be silence, teaching or creative activity and the singing of the following (to the tune Bunessan*) or another song*

Touch the earth lightly, use the earth gently,
nourish the life of the world in our care.
Gift of great wonder, ours to surrender,
trust for the children tomorrow will bear.
We who endanger, who create hunger;
agents of death for all creatures that live;

we who would foster clouds of disaster,
God of the planet, forestall and forgive.

Let there be greening, birth from the burning,
water that blesses and air that is sweet;
health in God's garden, hope in God's children,
regeneration that peace will complete.
God of all living, God of all loving,
God of the seedling, the soil and the sun,
teach us, deflect us, Christ reconnect us,
using us gently, making us one.

Intercession

Reader   Dear Creator,
teach us to care for your earth,
and to be good stewards of all that is in it.
May our eyes be open to see your hand in nature;
may our hands be open to cherish your gifts
in the material things around us;
may we learn how to live in harmony
with your laws.

Reader   Bless the soil on which we live, work
and make community.
May it bring forth goodness
to nourish and renew the whole community
who share it.
You made the earth and through the long ages
planted it with every kind of plant;
you made animals to crawl and to run upon it,
birds to fly over it and fish to swim around it.

When all was prepared,
you formed humankind from the soil.
You breathed your life into them.
May we never forget that we are mortal creatures;
from earth we come,
to earth we go.

Leader As the sun circles the world,
circle this land, O God,
circle the soil and the waters.
Keep harm without.
Keep good within.
Circle the crops, circle the homes.
Keep neglect without.
Keep care within.

There may be circling with the feet or hands
There may be free prayer and singing

Leader May the sun shine upon you and warm your heart
till it glows like a great fire,
so that a stranger as well as a friend
may be warmed by it.
May the blessing of the Sun of suns be on you,
giving you light without and light within,
so that the light shines out of your eyes.
May the blessing of the rain and the earth
and the wind be on you.
May the blessing of the Three-without-end
pour always graciously on you.

Night Prayer for Summer

Leader   The sun rides high and long,
a sign of blessing from our God.
Everything that breathes cries 'Yes!'
At day's fading we cry 'Yes' to Christ,
the eternal Sun.

All   Light of the world, in grace and beauty;
mirror of God's eternal face;
transparent flame of love's free duty –
you bring salvation to our race.
Now, as we see the sun is setting,
we raise our voice in songs of praise.
Worthy are you of endless blessing,
Sun of our night, light of our days.

There may be singing

Reader   The heavens bespeak the glory of God;
the firmament ablaze, a text of God's works.
Dawn whispers to sunset,
dark to dark the word passes: glory, glory.
All in a great silence, no tongue's clamour –
yet the web of the world trembles,
conscious, as of great winds passing.
The bridegroom's tent is raised; a cry goes up:
He comes! Rejoicing, presiding, his wedding day.
From end to end of the universe his progress.
No creature, no least being but catches fire
from him.

From Psalm 19, paraphrase by Daniel Berrigan

Leader	The beauty of summer, its days long and slow;
All	beautiful, too, visiting the ones we love.
Leader	The beauty of the garden when the leeks grow well;
All	beautiful, too, the charlock in blossom.
Leader	The beauty of the fish in his bright lake;
All	beautiful, too, its surface shimmering.
Leader	The beauty of flowers on the tops of fruit-trees;
All	beautiful, too, covenant with the Creator.

The Loves of Taliesin

Reader Jesus said 'I came in order that you may have
life – life in all its fullness.'

John 10:10

All Life of Jesus, Sun of suns, filling every part of us;
life be in our being and bloom be on our face
till you come back again.

Reader May our eyes be open to see your hand in nature.
May our hands be open to cherish your gifts.
May our hearts be open to love you in others.

*Examples of blessings of this long day may be
shared. There may be singing and free prayer for
the blessing of the land. The following or other
words may be read*

Praised be you, dear God, with all your creatures,
especially through Brother Sun,
who is the day, and through whom
you give us light.
He is beautiful and radiant, with great splendour,
and bears a likeness of you, Most High One.

325

Praised be you, my Lord, through Brother Wind,
and through the air, cloudy and serene,
and every kind of weather through which you
give sustenance to your creatures.
Praised be you, my Lord, through our sister,
Mother Earth,
who sustains and governs us,
and who produces varied fruits
with coloured flowers and herbs.

Praised be you, my Lord, for our nursemaid,
sleep, who calms and renews us,
and who restores us for the morrow.

Echoes Francis of Assisi's hymn

Leader   As the sun circles the earth, circle this land, O God:
circle the crops and the cattle,
the homes and all places of work.
Keep ill-will without and compassion within.
Keep harm without and well-being within.

Leader   Circle our dear ones, O God, in every place
where they are, especially . . .

Names may be mentioned

All   We quieten our souls under the stillness of sky:
peace be upon our breath,
peace be upon our eyes,
peace be upon our heart.

Leader   May the sun shine upon us and warm our hearts
till they glow like great fires.

May Christ, the Sun of suns,
give us light without and light within.
May the Three of love pour graciously upon us
as we sleep.

All sing

To the Sun of suns come singing,
Jesus is Lord. (*x 3*)
Earth come to the sun's King singing,
Jesus is Lord. (*x 3*)
Sky come to the sun's King singing,
Jesus is Lord. (*x 3*)
Spirits come to sun's King singing,
Jesus is Lord. (*x 3*)
Father, Saviour, lighting Spirit,
you are the Lord. (*x 3*)

Creative Activities for Summer

1. Body-and-soul prayer exercises.

2. Open-air sports, such as swimming, cycling or walking.

3. Picnic with music.

4. Dance.

5. Pick summer fruits and enjoy a fruity tea.

6. Display photographic or computer projections of the glories of the sun.

Autumn or Thanksgiving

This is a time of thanksgiving for God's goodness to our land through the memory and harvesting of both material and spiritual riches.

In the Celtic tradition three months of harvest celebrations concludes with the harvest of berries and nuts on 2 November.

The term 'Thanksgiving' reflects the US custom of linking gratitude for the completed harvest with thanksgiving for God's hand in its history, especially for its founding Christian pilgrims.

In Jewish tradition this is the Festival of Tabernacles or Shelters. Those who wish to reflect this may put up tents or shacks in a garden or a space next to their house for several days, and eat a meal there or sleep in it.

In the northern hemisphere this takes place in October; in the southern hemisphere it takes place in April.

Morning Prayer for
Autumn or Thanksgiving

Leader	Harvester God, as autumn light ripens the grain,
All	ripen too our souls.
Leader	As brown leaves fall and sheaves are stored,
All	help us to leave behind summer's ways
	and go forward in deepening compassion,
	thankful to heaven.

Thanksgiving

There may be singing

Reader	You are the life and hope of the earth.
	By your strength you established the mountains.
All	Let us bless our generous God whose goodness
	crowns the year.
Reader	You silence the roaring of waves and sea.
	You silence the tumult of the peoples.
	Those who live at earth's furthest bounds
	are awed by your signs.
All	Let us bless our generous God whose goodness
	crowns the year.
Reader	You make the gateways of the morning
	and evening shout for joy.
	You visit the earth and water it,
	you greatly enrich it.
	The river of God is full of water.
	You provide the people with grain
	you have prepared.

	You soften the earth with showers
	and bless its growth.
All	Let us bless our generous God
	whose goodness crowns the year.
Reader	You crown the year with your goodness;
	your ways overflow with richness.
	The desert pastures overflow,
	the meadows gird themselves with flocks,
	the valleys deck themselves with grain –
	they shout and sing together for joy.
All	Let us bless our generous God whose goodness
	crowns the year.

From Psalm 65

Leader	The Lord crowns the year with goodness:
All	let all creation give God praise.
Leader	With corn and flour and dairy we sing to God:
All	let all creation give God praise.
Leader	With berries, fruits and earth's flowered gems:
All	let all creation give God praise.
Leader	With beasts of land and sea we sing to God:
All	let all creation give God praise.
Leader	With birds' mirth and sun's glory
	we sing to God:
All	let all creation give God praise.
Leader	With wind and storm and purple deeps:
All	let all creation give God praise.
Leader	With those who fish and farm and trade:
All	let all creation give God praise.
Leader	With spirits and faithful souls
	who served these parts:
All	let all creation give God praise.

Lament

Leader	Father, the good things of your earth shout out your praise. Forgive us that our lives so seldom speak of gratitude.
All	Father, have mercy.
Leader	Lord, these good things are denied to people in other parts of your earth. Forgive us for pollution, neglect and greed.
All	Christ, have mercy.
Leader	Spirit, these good things would not be here unless their seeds of life had first lain still in the rhythms of winter's soil. Forgive us for trying to be what we are not and for resisting your rhythms.
All	Spirit, have mercy.

There may be silence or music

God's Word

Reader	Exodus 23:14-26
Leader	This we know: the earth does not belong to us;
All	we belong to the earth.
Leader	This we know: all things are connected,
All	like the blood that unites one family.
Leader	This we know: we did not weave the web of life;
All	we are merely a strand in it.

332

Leader	This we know: whatever we do to the web,
All	we do to ourselves.

Leader	Let us give thanks for the gift of creation.
All	Let us give thanks that all things hold together in Christ.

Reader	John 6:26-35; Joel 2:21-27
	or 1 Thessalonians 5:12-24

There may be singing, teaching, or creative activity such as the following

Leader	Without water no plants would grow.
All	Blessed be God for ever.

Leader	Without water no humans could live.
All	Blessed be God for ever.

Leader	Without water, the earth could never have been.
All	Blessed be God for ever.

Water may be brought in a container. Three representatives – perhaps persons in young, mid and old age – hold out their hands, and water is poured over them

Leader	May the life of God pour through you and through this land.

or

Offerings are made. People might, for example, bring food, mobile phones and such like and place them in a circle on a table

Leader   Lord, we pray for . . .
those whose crops have failed;
whose land has been ravaged by war;
the hungry, refugees, the homeless;
those whose harvest comes only after a constant
struggle with the elements;
all who plan for the resources of the earth;
that they may be shared.

Leader   Great Spirit,
Penetrate the storehouse of our memories,
making them whole and holy.
Bring to harvest the fragments of our lives
and crown our year with goodness.

Midday Prayer for Autumn or Thanksgiving

Reader   O sacred season of autumn, be my teacher,
for I wish to learn the virtue of contentment
as I gaze upon your full-coloured beauty.
I sense all about you an at-home-ness
with your amber riches.
You are the season of retirement,
of full barns and harvested fields.
The cycle of growth has ceased
and the busy work of giving life is now completed.
I sense in you no regrets;
for you have lived a full life.

Reader   Earth-maker God,
our society is ever restless,
always craving one more thing to do,
seeking happiness through more and more
possessions.
Teach us to be at peace with what we have,
to embrace what we have received,
to know that enough is enough
until our strivings cease
and we rest content in you alone.

Leader   O God, who called all life into being,
All   the earth, sea and sky are yours.

Leader   Your presence is all around us,
All   every atom is full of your energy.

Leader	Your Spirit enlivens all who walk on earth.
All	With her we yearn for justice to be done,
Leader	for creation to be freed from bondage,
All	for the hungry to be fed,
Leader	for captives to be released,
All	for your kingdom to come on earth.

Leader	Lord, make us co-workers with you
All	that humankind may reap a full harvest.
Leader	Lord, we pray for this world you have given us:
	for the planting of seeds;
	for the propagation of stock and fish,
	mining and drilling;
	for the birth of new ideas.
	We remember before you, Lord,
	those who cannot plant
	because hunger has driven them to eat the seed;
	and those whose animals are diseased and dying.
Leader	Lord, make us co-workers with you
All	that humankind may reap a full harvest.

Leader	Lord of the shadows, Lord of the day,
	Lord of the elements, Lord of the grey,
	Lord of creation, Lord of the way,
	grant us sureness in the nearness of your clasp.

Evening Prayer for
Autumn or Thanksgiving

Leader   Bountiful God,
seedtime has ripened into harvest,
your earth has yielded fruits.
Winter's cleansing cold
gave way to spring's gentle warmth,
and now summer's full sun
has offered us autumn gifts.

All   Giver of all, we come to worship you.

Leader   God of goodness,
the wonders of your creation,
the splendour of the heavens,
the order and richness of nature,
speak to us of your glory.
The coming of your Son,
the presence of your Spirit,
the fellowship of your Church,
show us the marvel of your love.
The patterns of the year,
the beauty of the earth,
the ripening gifts of harvest,
call us to worship and adore you.

There may be singing

Reader   Psalm 67

Leader   O God of Life, darken not to me your light.
All   O God of life, close not to me your joy.

| **Leader** | O God of Life, shut not to me your door. |
| **All** | O God of life, crown me with your gladness. |

Reader Thank you for those
who have upheld noble values,
exercised good judgement,
guided the uncertain.

Reader Thank you for the landscape of many deepening
hues,
the migration of bird flocks.

Reader Lord of the leaves and the land,
open the gate to plenty, to ripening fruit and grain,
to the maturing of wisdom.

God's Word

Reader Deuteronomy 8:7-18

All I believe, O God of all gods,
that you are the eternal Creator of life.
I believe, O God of all gods,
that you are the eternal Father of love.
I believe, O Lord and God of the peoples,
that you are the Creator of the high heavens.
I believe, O Lord and God of the peoples,
that you created my soul and set its warp.

Reader Mark 6:30-44

*There may be singing, silence, sharing, teaching
or a creative activity*

Thanksgiving

Leader   Creator, from whom come all good things,
we savour your presence and recall your
generosity towards us.

There may be a pause

Our hearts are grateful
for the life you have given us
and the world in which we live;
All   for the beauty and bounty of the world,
its seasons and its gifts;
Leader   for harvest's boundless store,
and the fruits of the earth that sustain
and gladden us;
All   for those who work the land,
or who are part of the food chain
that reaches our door;
Leader   for comforts of life,
for homes and fellowship,
and for the power to help others;
All   for your creation,
and the One you sent to restore us
when we fell away from your plan.

Leader   Your blessing on those who are entering retirement
and on those who have lost employment;
on women who are past childbearing;
on creatures who are trapped or in pain.
Your blessing on the wild and untamed places
of the planet.

There may be free prayer and singing

Leader   May this season of mellow fruitfulness
enrich and bless you.
May you harvest relationships of trust,
forgiveness and generosity.
And, until we meet again,
may you be kept in the hollow of God's hand.

Night Prayer for Autumn or Thanksgiving

Leader   At this sacred season of harvesting
and contentment,

All   we are content to be in your presence.

Leader   Through your providence, Lord, the earth has
yielded its fruit.

All   Tonight we yield ourselves to you.

Bread is placed on a dish

Reader   Be gentle when you touch bread.
Let it not lie, uncared for, unwanted.
So often bread is taken for granted.
There is such beauty in bread –
beauty of sun and soil,
beauty of patient toil.
Wind and rain have caressed it,
Christ often blessed it.
Be gentle when you touch it.

Anon

All   O God, who put ear in corn,
and skill and love in human hands
that make and hold this bread,
you are the Rock from which all earth
is fashioned,
you are the Food from which all souls are fed.
You, who put food in ear and herd,
you, who put fish in stream and sea,
put a glory in our sleep.

Reader	Psalm 67

Leader	Blessed be God, the Giver of light.
All	Blessed be God, the Provider of warmth.
Leader	Blessed be God, the Dispeller of darkness.
All	Blessed be God, the Giver of sleep.

Reader Maker of all,
teach us how to treat your world
with the respect it needs and deserves;
teach us to observe the rhythms and balance
of nature;
teach us to be one with you tonight.

Reader Matthew 13:24-30, John 4:32-36
or 2 Corinthians 9:6-10

Leader Your dear ones bless, O God, in every place.
Bring to completion
that which you have begun in them.
Work in these whom we name before you now.

Any may mention names

Leader May the Spirit stroke your brow
as weary down to sleep you go.
May the Father mark your rest,
empower you tomorrow to give your best.

All We'll sleep in the contentment of work well done.
We'll sleep in the ripeness of joy.

Leader Sleep in peace.
Sleep soundly.
Sleep in love.
Weaver of dreams,
weave well in you as you sleep.

Reader   Wisdom,
            come in to the storehouse of our memories.
            Be present through the silent hours
            and bring us safely to your glorious light.
            Lighten our darkness at the end of the day.
            Defend us from perils, our fears allay.
            Lighten our burdens, bring joy to our rest,
            and grant, on our waking, we give you our best.

Leader   At the drawing in of the day
            may your contemplations bring you peace.
            May the soft mists of God's presence
            wrap you in their gentle folds.
            May the light of God's presence lengthen you.
            May the might of God's presence strengthen you.
            May the warmth of God's presence restore you.
            May all that God has sowed in your life,
            flower and ripen.
            May God's harvest in your life be fruitful
            and abundant.

Echoes Blessings from Rock Community Church,
Dunbarton, Scotland, 2000

Creative Activities for Autumn or Thanksgiving

1. Bring examples of trees or plants that typically grow close to water.

2. Bring and display berries.

3. Bring examples of your life's experience over the last year or years, which now you wish to gather together and savour.

4. Make and/or give thanksgiving cards.

Winter

In the ancient Celtic calendar, winter (Samhain) was the three months from 1 November, and was the beginning of the year. It is appropriate to use these patterns of prayer on any day during this season.

Daily Winter Candle-lighting

These short liturgies may be used in households, or in churches before Evening or Night Prayer

In the northern hemisphere winter candle-lightings may begin at All Saints (1 November) and end at Candlemas (1 February), and may intersperse with candle-lightings for All Saints, Advent, Christmas and Epiphany (see pages 394, 144, 180 and 222 respectively in Volume One of the *Celtic Prayer Book*)

Reader   We bless you, Sovereign God,
        our light and our salvation.
        You led your people to freedom
        through a cloud by day and by fire at night.
        We give you thanks, Kindly Light,
        that you ever lead your people on.
        Light up our dark hearts
        by the light of your Christ.
        May his word illumine our way.

Reader   Spirit of the risen Christ,
        light up the darkness,
        shine into our hearts
        and kindle in us the fire of your love.

        A candle is lit

Reader   Jesus, co-Creator with the Father,
All   you light up our darkness.
Reader   Jesus, Fount of Eternal Wisdom,
All   you light up our darkness.

Reader If you walk in the light,
          you will have fellowship with one another.
All   We will walk in the light of your presence.
          We will follow your Christ,
          rising victorious as he scatters the darkness
          from our path.
          Amen.

Morning Prayer for Winter

Leader   Creator God,
whose power and beauty are never spent,
in wintry earth waken us to the mystery
of your Presence.

Thanksgiving

There may be singing

Reader   Psalm 147

Leader   Wind and storm, praise our King.
All   Frost and snow, praise our King,
Leader   Hard earth and whirring engines,
praise our King.
All   Mail and airwaves, praise our King.

God's Word

Reader   Job 37:2-12

Leader   We arise today,
All   in the deep gestation of winter,
in the transforming power of ice,
in the cleansing work of frost.

Leader   We arise today,
All   in the simplicity of the bare earth,
in the strength of the fierce elements,
in the beauty of snow-clad land.

Reader   Acts 28:1-11a

There may be teaching, creative activity and singing

Intercession

Leader   Stripped of inessentials we stand, rooted in you.
In the anticipation of gathering strength
you sustain our well-being.
In the stillness of the dark hours
we invite you to do your work in us.

Reader   Give us the humility of the bare earth.
Help us to place into your hands winter's
patterns, which you call us now to live.

There may be silence or free prayer

Leader   Thank you for a roof over our head,
for firm earth under our tread,
for supplies to fill our hunger,
for friends to assuage our anger.

There may be singing

Leader   At the drawing in of the year,
may your contemplations bring you peace,
may the wintry hardness of God's strength
make you strong,
and may the soft mists of God's presence
wrap you in their gentle folds.

Dunbarton Rock Community Church,
Scotland, 1998

Midday Prayer for Winter

Leader In the chill of wintry wind,
in the depths of uncertain thoughts,
sing to us the story of the universe;
visit us as Saviour of our being.

Pause

Leader Father,
be with us in every experience of life.
When we neglect you,
All remind us of your presence;
Leader when we are frightened,
All give us courage;
Leader when we are tempted,
All give us power to resist;
Leader when we are anxious and worried,
All give us peace;
Leader when we are weary in service,
All give us energy.

Reader Genesis 8:20-22

Leader We bind to ourselves this day
All the strength of rock,
the silence of earth,
the sharpness of cold.

Leader We bind to ourselves this day,
All the longevity of stars,
the integrity of sky,
the sobriety of darkness.

Reader	John 10:22-30

There may be free or silent prayer, the Lord's Prayer and singing.

Leader
All
Bless, O generous God,
our every action,
our every thought,
our every utterance.

Leader
All
Keep us, O Son of loveliest Mary,
from evil wish,
from idle chatter,
from foolish deed.

Leader
Hold us, O God of the cold, dark days
secure in the knowledge that,
from its wintry depths,
the earth brings forth a Saviour.
All
Amen.

Evening Prayer for Winter

Leader Creating and Sustaining God,
as this cold, dark season encroaches,
give to us the stability of the deep earth
and the hope of heaven.

Reader Thank you for guiding us to this time
of briefest light,
All secure in the trust that you embrace
the encircling gloom;
Leader held by the dark which you encompass
in your arms,
All content to rest in you like a baby in the womb.

There may be singing

God's Word

Reader Psalm 74:10-21

Leader Counsellor,
quicken my soul's progress in this winter season.
Kindle in me the heart-fires of welcome and love
All in the presence of the Holy Trinity,
in the presence of the angels, without envy,
in the presence of the saints, without fear.

Reader Job 37:1-13

There may be silence or singing

Leader When your icing coats the world,
All it gives us such pleasure.
Leader When you send snow and frost and dew,
All it is like walking on jewels.

Leader	And when it is just damp and dark
All	it teaches us to wait.

Pause

Reader Acts 28:1-9

There may be teaching, creative activity and singing

Intercession

Leader In our weakness, winter reveals to us
our true strength:
strength to be broken,
strength to be still.
In you alone, O God, can our true life begin.

There may be silence and chanting

Leader Out of the womb of darkness
leapt the Everlasting Light.
We enter the womb of darkness
knowing it is yours, dear Lord.
We bring to you, our Nurturer,
our fears and the despair of the world.

Any may mention examples of people in despair

There may be singing

Leader As the holly bears the berries rich-red and deep,
though all around seems bare,
so may you bear the fruits of God working
deeply in your life.

Night Prayer for Winter

Psalm 134 or 139:1-12 may be read or the
following words of Psalm 134 may be sung or said

All   Come bless the Lord, all you servants of the Lord
who stand by night in the house of the Lord;
lift up your hands in the holy place.
Come bless the Lord, come bless the Lord.

Leader   Star-kindler and Weaver of wonder,
as winter stars light up the darkness of night,
reveal to us fresh sources of hope.

Candles may be lit

Leader   When cold night draws near,
All   we draw near to you.
Leader   When dark cares loom large,
All   we draw near to you.
Leader   In our hard place of need,
All   we draw near to you.
Leader   Clothe us in garments whiter than snow,
and warm us to love your Word.

Reader   1 John 2:7-14

There may be silence or sharing of other Bible texts

Leader   Come, Protector of heaven and earth,
and cover us with night.
Spread your grace over us.
Your promises are more than the stars in the sky.

Night comes with the cold,
and with the breath of death.
Your mercy is deeper than the night.
Night comes, the end comes,
you come.

Echoes a prayer from Ghana

Males   I place my soul and body
under your guiding this night, O Christ.
O Son of the journey through darkness,
may your cross this night be my shield.

Females   I place my soul and body
under your glowing this night, O Spirit,
O gentle Companion and soul Guardian,
my heart's eternal Warmth.

There may be singing

Leader   You are our Saviour and Lord,
All   in our stumbling be our Shield.
Leader   In our tiredness be our Rest.
All   In our darkness be our Light.

Leader   Your dear ones bless, O God, wherever they are;
especially these we name before you now.

Any may name dear ones and others

Leader   Be their Companion and ours
as we wait this night.

All   In time of cold may we find warmth in you.
In time of trial may we find Love Divine.
In time of dark may we find everlasting Light.

Acknowledgements

The author and publishers wish to thank the following for kind permission to reproduce their copyright material:

Ateliers et Presses de Taizé, 71250 Taizé Community, France, for the text 'Within our darkest night', from Jacques Berthier, *Songs and Prayers from Taizé*.

Ian Fosten, for the prayer 'Dear Father God', from an awareness trail leaflet produced for the St Cuthbert Centre (URC), Holy Island.

Brian Frost, for 'May we be bold in the love of God', from *Poems of Grief and Glory* (New World Publications 2002), p. 78.

Susan Howatch, for 'What exactly is healing?', based on a speech on the ministry of healing given at Holy Trinity Church, Sloane Street, London, in November 1997.

Oxford University Press, for the prayer by George Appleton, from *The Oxford Book of Prayer*, p. 257, George Appleton (ed), (Oxford, 2002).

Ian Silk, for the prayer 'Lord, these your little ones'. The author is currently Vicar of St George's Church, Swallowbeck, Lincoln.